Furniture + Architecture

Guest-edited by Edwin Heathcote

WILEY-ACADEMY

AD

Architectural Design
Vol 72 No 4 July 2002

Editorial Offices
International House
Ealing Broadway Centre
London W5 5DB
T: +44 (0)20 8326 3800
F: +44 (0)20 8326 3801
E: architecturaldesign@wiley.co.uk

Editor
Helen Castle
Executive Editor
Maggie Toy
Production
Mariangela Palazzi-Williams
Art Director
Christian Küsters ↘ CHK Design
Designer
Yumiko Tahata ↘ CHK Design
Picture Editor
Famida Rasheed

Advertisement Sales
01243 843272

Editorial Board
Denise Bratton, Adriaan Beukers,
André Chaszar, Peter Cook,
Max Fordman, Massimiliano
Fuksas, Anthony Hunt, Charles
Jencks, Jan Kaplicky, Robert
Maxwell, Jayne Merkel, Monica
Pidgeon, Antoine Predock,
Leon van Schaik

Contributing Editors
Craig Kellogg
Jeremy Melvin

ISBN 0-47084568-6
Profile No 158

Abbreviated positions
b=bottom, c=centre, l=left, r=right

Front cover image by James Harris.
Barcelona Chair by Mies van der Rohe,
in front of a plastic wall by Inflate.
Back cover image:
6a, light, 2001, photo Jim Colley

∆ main section
p 4 © Richard Wentworth; p 6(l) © Richard
Glover/VIEW; p 6(r) courtesy B & B Italia; pp
7, 8 & 10-12 photographs courtesy The
National Trust, 2 Willow Road; pp 9 & 13
RIBA Library Photographs Collection; pp 14
& 16 Archive Vitra Design Museum; pp 17,
18(b) & 19-21 courtesy Edwin Heathcote; p
18(t) © DACS 2002; pp 22, 24 & 25 © Sarah
Jackson; p 23 courtesy Akehurst Bureau,
photo © Lewis Morley; pp 26, 30 & 31(t)
Ezra Stoller © Esto; p 27(t) courtesy
Diller+Scofidio, © Michael Moran; p 27
(bl&r) courtesy of Cranbrook Archives; p
32(b) © Björg Arnarsdottir; p 32(t&r) photo
© Chuck Choi; pp 34-7 courtesy of
chanceprojects.com, © Neil Cummings; p
38 © Duccio Malagamba-fotographia de
arquitectura; p 39 courtesy Edwin
Heathcote, © Álvaro Siza, Portugal; p 40
courtesy Vitra, photo Richard Bryant; pp 42-
3 & 45 courtesy John Pawson; pp 42 &
43(tl&r) © AG Fronzoni, p 43(b) © Cindy
Palmano, p 45(t) photography by AG
Fronzoni and p 45(b) photo Ian Dobbie; p 44
courtesy Maarten van Severen furniture
produced by tm; pp 46-53 courtesy Adjaye
Associates: p 46(l) photo Brigitte Bouillot,
pp 46(r), 50 & 52(tl&r, br) & 53(tl&b) photo
© Lyndon Douglas and pp 47-9 & 51(t&bl)
photo © Ed Reeve; pp 54, 55(b), 57(cl&r),
60, 62(tr&b) © Alison Brooks Architects; p
55(t) & 56(b) courtesy Alison Brooks; p 56(t)

© Ron Arad Associates; pp 58 & 59
courtesy Jam; pp 61-62(tl) © Dennis
Gilbert/VIEW; pp 63-71 courtesy Gans &
Jelacic: pp 63, 64, 65 (tl,tr&bl), 66 & 67 ©
Gans & Jelacic, p 65 (m&br) photo Susan
Swider, pp 68-9 © AC2 Studio, p 70 photo
© Robert Barnstone and p 71 © R+Design;
pp 72-7 courtesy 6A: p 72 photo Jim Colley
and pp 76(l) & 77(tr) photos David
Grandorge; pp 78-9 photos © Chris
Pommer, PLANT; p 80 courtesy Susan
Grant Lewin, © A: D/B project space, photo
John Barrons; pp 81-3 © Ali Tayar, photos
Joshua McHugh; pp 84-6 photographs from
the Isokon Plus Archive; pp 91(t) & 94(br) ©
Selfridges & Co; pp 90 & 94(t&bl) courtesy
Future Systems © Richard Davies; p 92 ©
Ron Arad Associates; p 92(br) © Ron Arad
Associates, photo Perry Hagopian; p 95
courtesy Knoll International Ltd; p 96
courtesy Kartell.

∆+ section
p 98+ courtesy Charles Jencks, photo ©
Lily Jencks; p 100+ © courtesy Charles
Jencks © Dokumentation Le Corbusier,
Stiftung Heidi Weber, Zürich; pp 102-6+
courtesy of Eisenman Architects; pp 107,
108(t), 108(bl&r)+ © Elizabeth Felicella; pp
108(c) & 109+ © Renzo Piano Building
Workshop/Fox & Fowle Architects;
pp 110-15+ © OCEAN NORTH; pp 116+ &
118+ © Max Fordham LLP; p 119+ Peter
Cook/VIEW; p 120(t)+ The Collection of The
Earl of Pembroke, Wilton House, Salisbury,
UK; p 120(b)+ © Dennis Gilbert/VIEW; p
121(b)+ Paxton Locher Architects; pp 122-
4+ courtesy Dominique Perrault Architecte:
pp 122+ & 123(tr)+ photo André Morin;
p 125+ courtesy Johnson Chou Design,
photos Volker Seding.

Subscription Offices UK
John Wiley & Sons Ltd.
Journals Administration Department
1 Oldlands Way, Bognor Regis
West Sussex, PO22 9SA
T: +44 (0)1243 843272
F: +44 (0)1243 843232
E: cs-journals@wiley.co.uk

Subscription Offices USA and Canada
John Wiley & Sons Ltd.
Journals Administration Department
605 Third Avenue
New York, NY 10158
T: +1 212 850 6645
F: +1 212 850 6021
E: subinfo@wiley.com

Annual Subscription Rates 2001
Institutional Rate: UK £160
Personal Rate: UK £99
Student Rate: UK £70
Institutional Rate: US $240
Personal Rate: US $150
Student Rate: US $105

∆ is published bi-monthly.
Prices are for six issues and include
postage and handling charges.
Periodicals postage paid at Jamaica,
NY 11431. Air freight and mailing in the
USA by Publications Expediting Services
Inc, 200 Meacham Avenue, Elmont,
NY 11003

Single Issues UK: £22.50
Single Issues outside UK: US $36.00
Order two or more titles and postage
is free. For orders of one title ad
£2.00/US $5.00. To receive order
by air please add £5.50/US $10.00

Postmaster
Send address changes to ∆ Publications
Expediting Services, 200 Meacham Avenue,
Elmont, NY 11003

Printed in Italy. All prices are subject
to change without notice.
[ISSN: 0003-8504]

Furniture + Architecture

Guest-edited by Edwin Heathcote

AD

Architect-designed furniture provides the interiors' world with its own fashion labels. People as enthusiastically covet a Barcelona or Swan chair as they might a pair of Prada shoes. Such a thriving collector's and reproduction market for modern classic designs can only be a boon to architecture, feeding interest and broadening cultural references. It also, as we decided at △, begs review: how should the relationship between furniture and architecture be constructed? How is it shifting? To look at such a relationship, it is necessary to include classic designers – Ernö Goldfinger, Mies van der Rohe, Arne Jacobsen, Eero Saarinen and Max Bill. To understand their intentions and then again to see how they are currently being reinterpreted. (This crossover is most apparent in Jayne Merkel's essay on Saarinen when she shows the No 71 Knoll side chairs reupholstered in white leather for Diller & Scofidio's Brasserie in New York.) The project for a 'total design' philosophy is grown by those such as Alvaro Siza, John Pawson and David Adjaye, only to be playfully prodded by a new generation of designers. Tom Emerson of 6A displays the ultimate confidence, illustrating his brilliant door-stopper/door-handle design with a drawing of a Georgian door! △

When Mies's Barcelona chairs or early original models or prototypes of Breuer's tubular furniture come up for sale, they are put in the Decorative Arts sales of the big international auction houses. Decorative art? What could be less decorative or more functional than a Functionalist chair? The answer, of course, is that the furniture of the bourgeois/intellectual/aesthete home is, perhaps surprisingly, very little to do with function.

Architect-designed furniture is the status symbol par excellence, it has become art-furniture. The Barcelona chair and Corb's cubic black-leather armchair have long been the most lasting features of the corporate lobby, but now the Eames chair and ottoman are the centrepiece of the cultured living room (think of Frasier's smug condo), Jacobsen's Butterfly chair the only splash of organic shaping in thousands of developers' minimalist kitchens and dining rooms, and Corb's lounger the focus of ads for lifestyle products, cars, penthouse developments and insurance.

These products have attained a ubiquity and recognisability (and availability) which their designers' architecture has rarely managed. The originals of these cult objects have become highly sought-after artworks, bought as investments like paintings and placed in museums and collections around the world. But these are not artworks. They are chairs, made of affordable industrial materials, to be sat in. By transposing them into the context of a museum the everyday is made exclusive and this affects the whole idea of design. Furniture is now designed with the museum in mind as much as, or more than, the user. This is often leading to outrageous or whimsical shapes, to psychedelic splashes of colour and 'limited editions' (Neil Cummings calls it 'Look at me!') or to a caricatured functionalism, but to few good pieces of furniture which are likely to last. Of course, what this museumification does for the designer is indisputable. It confers upon the industrial designer or the architect the status of artist. Art, of course, does not have to work. Chairs do. There is remarkably little common ground between art and industrial design or architecture yet their cultural status is getting ever closer.

The natural environment for modern furniture is the home, the corporate lobby or the shop – why go to a museum to see pieces of furniture which can be seen for free in a designer furniture showroom? In fact, it could be argued that the heavy involvement of architects in the design of retail environments creates a better setting. John Pawson's showroom for B&B Italia

in London's Brompton Road is in the tradition of Marcel Breuer's still extant (and still exemplary) shop for Wohnbedarf in Zurich, and these shops remain among the best places to see new design, far better than the world's burgeoning design museums.

The notion of the design museum dates back at least to the Victorians, perhaps to the Great Exhibition and to Morris's reaction to the lack of 'taste' in the objects exhibited at the Crystal Palace. It is always a didactic and bourgeois project, for good design is aimed at the middle classes; the upper classes inherit their furniture; and the working class is left out of the debate altogether.

Many socially aware architects have, throughout the last decades of the 19th century and the first few of the 20th, been concerned with the provision of a universal good design, with the creation of mass-produced products which make good design accessible to the masses. But remarkably few have achieved any real progress.

Many socially aware architects have, throughout the last decades of the 19th century and the first few of the 20th, been concerned with the provision of a universal good design, with the creation of mass-produced products which make good design accessible to the masses. But remarkably few have achieved any real progress. Marcel Breuer's tubular chairs (themselves based on prototypes by Mart Stam) are a good example of the successes, so was the bentwood furniture designed by Josef Hoffmann for the Thonet company, versions of which remain a café staple.

One of the real problems here is the question of industrial design. Buildings, like utensils or furniture, have to be designed and have to work. But the parameters of the idea of 'function' for objects, furniture and so on are vastly different from those in architecture. If a chair is uncomfortable, it is a failure as a chair – although this of course would not stop it becoming a cult object. Think of Mackintosh's stylised ladder-backed chair, among the most famous pieces of architect-designed furniture – it is uncomfortable and poorly constructed. A building can be poorly designed and bodged up yet still be exactly what the client wants. Function (apart from stopping leaks, draughts, building collapse etc) is much harder to define in architecture than in a teapot, a chair or a spoon. Industrial designers are educated to design objects the sole function of which is to work. The Functionalist tradition indicates that if an object

Opposite
San Francisco, 2001,
Richard Wentworth.

'The sort of world they [Richard Wentworth and Neil Cummings] arer talking about is about people being resourceful and inventive beyond what is intended and suggested by the object.'
Tom Emerson, 6a (see: inerview on p. 76).

fate and, ultimately, the vitrine and the museum against which their designers were rebelling.

Contemporary design companies are now mass-producing 'design' objects aimed at a 'lifestyle' market. A nebulous shape is applied to a practical item to ascribe to it designer qualities, whether this be a computer or a toaster. The result is a plastic body which is far more the essence of the planned obsolescence railed against in the 1950s. Cubans are still famously cruising around in 1950s cars – products which were held to be the height of planned obsolescence but have proved more than capable of being patched up and repaired. It is hard to imagine someone using an i-mac or a Starck toilet brush, or most of the other contemporary icons in 50 years' time, even if their materials will last far longer than the metal bodies of those Cuban Cadillacs.

Modern design products (or most mass-production products) are not built to last, but built for fashion, designed to catch the eye on a shop shelf like the kitchen products in Neil Cummings' photos. They have no capacity for repair or for reuse. The result is that they lose the potential for new lives in new settings. They do not exist in the world of 'things' written about by Georges Perec, talked about by Tom Emerson and documented by Richard Wentworth and Neil Cummings. Their's is a shelf life, designed to be seen, not used, discarded and not reused. These objects cannot partake in change, they exist only in the limiting world of the present. Architects design (or should design) buildings to exist in a street, to be in the world as we dwell in them, and to be able to bear change, both outside and in.

Yet when it comes to product or furniture design, architects are primarily concerned with what those things look like. Think of chairs by Mario Botta, Le Corbusier, Mackintosh or Frank Lloyd Wright and you'll know what I mean. While these pieces of furniture may become style icons and crop up in design (decorative arts) auctions, they do little to advance the lives of people or ideas about design. They are designed to be displayed in design museums. They are designed to be extraordinary, not ordinary. This is the problem with the way our superstar designer system works. What I have tried to do in this volume is to balance the shelves-full of brightly coloured homages to brightly coloured chairs by bringing together a collection of essays on designers more interested in function, in use, in the ordinary and the everyday, and in the relationship of furniture to space than in how their pieces will look in the design museum. ☎

Above left
View of the B&B Italia showrooms in Brompton Road, London, previous to its fit-out. The structure was designed by John Pawson.

Above right
The B&B Italia showroom in London opened with its completed interior by Antonio Citterio and Partners and furniture in place.

works for that for which it was designed and is easily mass-produced, it is a success (there is here another whole story about objects that work for uses for which they were not designed). The aesthetic will grow out of the function. Of course we know this was not the case. The Bauhaus designers produced streams of impossibly elegant objects, the aim of which was to appear functional but which were, in fact, completely unsuited to mass-production and made almost entirely by hand. These were objects longing to be placed in the proletarian home, but destined for a bourgeois

Ernö Goldfinger
The Architect as Furniture Designer

Ernö Goldfinger (1902–87) devoted a significant part of his early career to designing furniture. Yet by the 1950s he had all but given this up to concentrate exclusively on architecture. This may be one reason why very little has been written about this aspect of his work.[1] Records of some 200 designs have survived and these reflect the true breadth of his interests. In this article, **Rebecca Milner** draws on these records to discuss Goldfinger's activities as a furniture designer and considers what influenced his designs and their relationship to his architecture.

Goldfinger began to design furniture in the late 1920s whilst still a student of architecture at the École Des Beaux Arts, Paris. His early designs were executed in association with fellow Hungarian, Andre Szivessy (1901–58) and heavily influenced by the functional style of European Modernism. Their main interest was in the development of standardised furniture for industrial production using modern materials such as tubular steel. Despite their efforts, however, production of the tubular steel designs was limited and usually related to specific apartment and shop interiors or exhibition stands such as that done for Alpina in 1928. During the four years that he worked with Szivessy, Goldfinger also took a particular

interest in storage and in 1927 entered a competition run by the Austrian bentwood furniture company, Thonet. His designs for Thonet included a clothes cupboard that had distinctive internal features for storing pressed shirts, shoes and laundry.

The 1920s were formative years for Goldfinger. In 1923 he met and interviewed Le Corbusier for a Hungarian newspaper and at the Exposition des Arts Dècoratifs of 1925 saw Le Corbusier's Pavilion de l'Esprit Nouveau. Goldfinger has acknowledged the impact of Le Corbusier's work on his architecture, and it is also evident in his furniture designs from this period.[2] For the Pavilion, Le Corbusier developed a range of storage units which could be combined in different configurations and could stand against a wall or be arranged back to back to divide the room into

areas with different functions.[3] Goldfinger's
own interest in the possibilities of built-in and
freestanding storage evolved steadily from the
late 1920s onwards. No doubt the design and
furnishing of his own apartments heightened
his awareness of the need for practical and
flexible furniture in small modern flats. Based
on the early designs for Thonet he developed
a new series of storage units for clothes,
books and linen. The units had tambour
fronts, a feature of Le Corbusier's designs,
and one which Goldfinger exploited for its
utility as well as its decorative appearance.
Goldfinger furnished several rooms of his
Paris apartment at 3 Rue de la Citè
Universitaire with combinations of these
units and, like Le Corbusier, exploited their
potential as internal walls or partitions.

The partnership with Szivessy ended in
1929 and after spending a year in Algeria
Goldfinger set up his own practice in Paris
in 1931, the same year that he completed his
architectural training. Interiors and furniture
constituted the bulk of his work and he
continued to design for production. The first
significant 'production piece' of his own was
a tubular steel stacking chair, model A41 or
Entas, literally 'the stacker', from the French
verb *entasser*, 'to stack'. Although it was
conceived as a standard type suitable for
mass production on a large scale, only
prototypes and relatively small batches of
the design appear to have been made. These
were for Goldfinger's own use or for the

apartments of his clients, and were made by the small
furniture company of Roger Bourdeaux, 38 Rue de Malte.
Goldfinger sometimes ordered standard pressed plywood
seats and backs from Thonet, but he failed to interest them
in larger-scale production of the chairs.[4] Such rejections,
however, did not deter him from continuing to develop the
Entas series, and he designed numerous variations
throughout the 1930s and 1940s.

The continued influence of Le Corbusier can be seen in
a chair designed by Goldfinger around 1930 – model A33 or
the Safari Chair. The source for Goldfinger's design was
the Roorkhee Campaign Chair, a hard-wearing collapsible
chair originally designed for British Army officers in India
and which was used more widely for hunting and camping.[5]
During the 1920s the English furniture manufacturer Maple
& Co was selling a version called the Indian Chair.
Goldfinger would have been familiar with this through
Le Corbusier who admired Maples furniture for its utility
and commercial success. He would also have known Le
Corbusier's own version of the campaign chair designed in
association with Charlotte Perriand in 1928. Theirs was a
more radical and sophisticated interpretation of the original
source. Whereas Goldfinger used the traditional materials
of leather, canvas and wood and made few changes to the
construction and form, Le Corbusier and Perriand exploited
tubular steel and incorporated a daring curved section
which seemingly disconnected the seat rails and back legs
at the normal point of contact.[6]

The aesthetic differences between Goldfinger's Safari
Chair and Le Corbusier's chair with pivoting back reflect
the contrasts to be found in the architecture of the two
men. In his buildings Goldfinger preferred to retain the
natural surfaces of materials such as brick, concrete and
wood. He also left structural elements such as rolled steel

joists (RSJS) exposed so that the construction of the building was revealed. This 'truth to materials' approach recalls the design philosophy of the Arts and Crafts movement and is expressed in the simple construction and traditional materials of the Safari Chair. Le Corbusier's buildings of the 1920s were characterised by their luminous white facades, a feature that emphasised their form and masked both the colour and texture of the concrete beneath. Although he did not hide the qualities of the materials in his furniture, Le Corbusier's preoccupation with form was evident in the distinct geometry of the designs and the sophisticated construction.

Despite its obvious associations with the outdoors, Goldfinger saw his Safari Chair as a domestic piece of furniture and had several made for his apartment in Paris. He also used them most notably in a house at Cucq, near Le Touquet in France. Called 'The Outlook' and commissioned by Monsieur and Madame Lahousse in 1933 this was Goldfinger's first complete building designed on Modernist principles. The interiors were functional and incorporated fitted furniture as well as light and flexible freestanding pieces. The living room was furnished with Safari chairs, as well as stools and tables in the same style. The choice of this outdoor/indoor furniture was entirely appropriate for a room where almost an entire wall was glazed. This glass 'wall' consisted of panels that could be opened or closed, giving the inhabitants the opportunity to engage with the external living space all year round.

Having completed his first building, when Goldfinger moved to London in 1934 he found that there were limited opportunities to design buildings on Modernist principles. The continental style was regarded as cold and austere by many critics and often misunderstood, as Goldfinger experienced when he applied for planning permission to build his house in Willow Road, Hampstead. These circumstances meant that for the first few years, in London at least, he continued to design mainly apartment and shop interiors as well as furniture. He developed a particularly fruitful relationship with Paul and Marjorie Abbatt, the owners of the educational toy manufacturer Abbatt Toys.

As well as two shop interiors, the Abbatts commissioned Goldfinger to design toys and furniture. He had had some previous experience of designing for children and this was an opportunity to develop his designs further.

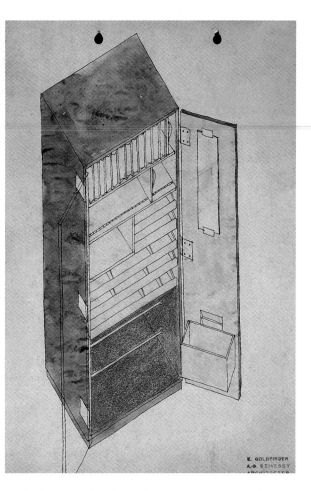

He had a young family of his own at the time and so perhaps was designing for them as much as for children in general. Based on his Entas and Safari chairs, Goldfinger designed seating that came in three sizes appropriate for children of different ages. Further concessions to children included the painting of the metal frames of the Entas-style chairs in different colours and a choice of coloured canvas upholstery for the Safari-style chairs. He also designed tables and storage units for toys and books as well as a new 'nesting' or stacking chair made entirely of plywood (1937). This chair also came in three sizes and had a pivoting back similar to the Entas. It is possible that Goldfinger was inspired by a plywood stacking chair designed by Marcel Breuer for Isokon around 1936.

Goldfinger continued to refine his designs for storage and in 1937 he was approached by the fitted kitchen specialist Easiwork, regarding furniture for an All-in Bungalow to be exhibited at the Ideal Home show at Olympia. The Bungalow was aimed at the 'week-ender', 'pensioner', and 'all those who appreciate the advantages of inexpensive living accommodation', and being small had to have space-saving flexible furniture.[7] Goldfinger incorporated by now characteristic features such as tambour fronts and interchangeable internal fittings into his designs. The marketing materials for the exhibition emphasised the architectural qualities of the furniture and the particular freedom it gave to the homeowner. The units were effectively a set of containers, hollow building blocks, which stood alone or fitted together. After the exhibition Goldfinger agreed to act as an adviser on the design and manufacture of the 'Easiwork Furniture Elements'. A catalogue was

produced, however, he made it difficult for the company to sell the units freely by insisting that all potential enquiries be referred to him. This arrangement meant that he could supply his own clients directly but by restricting the manufacturer he missed the opportunity of gaining wider commercial success with his designs.

Goldfinger adopted an austere masculine style that combined strong lines and cold smooth materials such as glass, steel and marble with the warmer tones and richer textures of waxed oak or mahogany. The overall effect was subdued luxury.

In Paris Goldfinger had met the Austrian Modernist Adolf Loos and during the mid-1930s continued to be inspired by Loos both in his choice of materials and his use of built-in furniture to articulate internal spatial divisions. Like Loos, Goldfinger adopted an austere masculine style that combined strong lines and cold smooth materials such as glass, steel and marble with the warmer tones and richer textures of waxed oak or mahogany. The overall effect was subdued luxury. A striking example of Goldfinger's assimilation of Loos's style is a sideboard now in the collection of the V&A. This piece was designed in 1935/6 for the home of his stockbroker, Mr Benroy, in Hendon, North London. It is constructed of mahogany faced on three sides with dark green veined marble. This juxtaposition of wood and marble can be seen in the library of Karma Villa, near Montreux, Switzerland, designed by Loos in 1904–06. In

Loos's design, the richness of the materials is tempered by the practicality of built-in shelving. It is possible that Goldfinger's sideboard was also a built-in feature – both this and its pair in the Wolfsonian in Florida show evidence of having at one time fitted around a structural element of the dining room for which it was designed.[8]

Goldfinger's most significant architectural project in the 1930s was the terrace of three houses in Willow Road. On completion of the building in 1939 he moved into number 2 with his family and lived there until his death in 1987. Apart from the practical built-in cupboards and shelving which is a distinct feature of the interiors at Willow Road, none of the other furniture appears to have been specifically designed for the house. The Goldfingers had brought furniture over from France including wardrobes and cupboards as well as Entas and Safari chairs, and these were used in their Highgate flat before becoming part of the furnishings at Willow Road.[9] Some of the furniture was adapted to new uses, for example the tambour-fronted wardrobe from the bedroom in Paris. No longer needed as a wardrobe, Goldfinger converted it into a cabinet for the living room by resting it horizontally on two sections of RSJ.

The table and sideboard in the dining room were amongst the newest pieces of furniture at Willow Road. Unlike his chair designs and unit furniture these were one-off pieces which were only reproduced for specific commissions. The most distinctive feature of the two pieces is the way they are supported – in the case of the table, the top rests on a cast iron machine tool base; two sections of RSJ form the 'legs' of the sideboard. Surrealism provides one context for interpreting these features.[10] The combination of RSJs with a practical cupboard and elaborate 19th-century candelabra (displayed on the top of the sideboard), for example, conveys both utility and grandeur. Juxtaposing seemingly unrelated objects in this way to convey opposing concepts was a favourite device of the Surrealists. Interpreted in the context of Modernism the metal supports also imbue the furniture with the idea of machine production, advanced technology and standardisation, and enhance its modern utilitarian appeal. Like his contemporaries Goldfinger was keen to express his Modernist ideals in the form and materials of his furniture even if it was made in more traditional ways and/or in limited numbers.

The sideboard was made by the cabinet-maker Andrew A Pegram and correspondence between the craftsman and the designer reveal the high standard of materials and workmanship that Goldfinger expected. Goldfinger wrote to Pegram to say that he could not accept the sideboard because the doors were too stiff and the linoleum on the top showed 'some regrettable imperfects'.[11] He demanded Pegram take it back and address the problems. Goldfinger's professional papers are testimony to many such exchanges; he would not

Footnotes
1. For a chronological survey of Goldfinger's architectural output see James Dunnett and Gavin Stamp, *Ernö Goldfinger*, Works 1 Architectural Association (London), 1983. A number of his furniture designs are reproduced in Robert Elwall, *Ernö Goldfinger*, RIBA Drawings Monographs No 3, Academy Editions (London), 1996, and Jill Lever, *Architects' Designs for Furniture*, RIBA Drawings Series, Trefoil Books (London), 1982.
2. See Elwall, op cit, p 10.
3. George H Marcus, *Le Corbusier: Inside the Machine for Living In*, Monacelli Press (New York), 2000, p 33.
4. Ernö Goldfinger Papers, Manuscripts and Archives Collection, British Architectural Library, RIBA, Ref Gol276\1.
5. See Nicholas A Brawer, *British Campaign Furniture: Elegance Under Canvas 1740–1914*, Harry N Abrams (New York), 2001, pp 70–73, and Clement Meadmore, *The Modern Chair: Classics in Production*, Studio Vista (London), 1974.
6. See Marcus, op cit, p 112.
7. See Ernö Goldfinger Papers, Manuscripts and Archives Collection, British Architectural Library, RIBA, Ref Gol466\7.
8. It is difficult to be sure exactly how the two sideboards fitted into the room, as only photographs of a third, similar, but wider sideboard from the same interior have survived.
9. See Ernö Goldfinger Papers, Manuscripts and Archives Collection, British Architectural Library, RIBA, Ref Gol278\2.
10. Goldfinger collected Surrealist art and knew several Surrealist artists. Alan Powers has discussed the role of surrealism in the modern house in his essay 'A Zebra at Villa Savoye: interpreting the Modern House', *The Modern House Revisited*, The Journal of the Twentieth Century Society, No 2, 1996.
11. See Ernö Goldfinger Papers, Manuscripts and Archives Collection, British Architectural Library, RIBA, Ref Gol277\6.
12. Ernö Goldfinger, *British Furniture Today*, Alec Tiranti (London), 1951, p 6.
13. Quote from 'Urbanism and spatial order' by Ernö Goldfinger. See Dunnett and Stamp, p 51.

rest (or pay!) until he was entirely satisfied. Was this insistence on furniture that was well made and of good materials an extension of his desire for permanence in his architecture? Certainly remarkably little 'new' furniture was ever bought or made for Willow Road over the 50 years or so that Goldfinger lived there. Often furniture was just repaired, refinished or altered.

Goldfinger spent the war years designing evacuation camps and prefabricated housing, as well as exhibitions for the Army Bureau of Current Affairs. He also wrote and published three important articles on the role of architecture in shaping and defining space to meet human needs. The restrictive economic climate continued for some years after the war and Goldfinger received very few architectural commissions, not even for interiors, and without this incentive appears to have all but given up designing furniture. By the 1950s both conditions and taste had changed, and Goldfinger's uncompromising style of architecture which had hitherto found little favour in Britain, was suddenly in demand. His practice began to flourish, and as the commissions for buildings increased he spent significantly less time designing furniture. There are records of nearly 200 designs dating from the 1920s, 1930s and 1940s, but little evidence of new designs after this date. Where he did have responsibility for interior furnishings he rarely used his own designs. In the French Government Tourist Office at 178 Piccadilly, London, for example, designed with Charlotte Perriand in 1963, Goldfinger used tables designed by his daughter Liz, easy chairs by a young furniture designer named Paul Goble and office furniture designed by Charles and Ray Eames.

Nevertheless, Goldfinger remained interested in furniture design. He often visited art college graduate shows and reviewed the work of young furniture designers for the architectural press. In 1951 he also wrote *British Furniture Today*, a brief guide to 'modern' furniture in Britain. The book featured some of his own designs from the 1930s alongside the work of younger designers such as Robin Day and Ernest Race. Given that he had failed to get his designs into wider production in Britain he perhaps saw this as an opportunity for self-promotion. It was also an opportunity to promote the Modernist principles that had informed his own designs such as mass production, modern materials, and design based on human needs.

In *British Furniture Today* Goldfinger identified independence from architectural form as a defining feature of modern furniture:

Furniture is now made for man and for his many needs, and no longer in accordance with formulae derived from the Five Orders of Architecture. It is made for human use, and not to go with the room for which it is designed.[12]

In the context of his own work, this was reflected in his pursuit of standardised furniture types, which were conceived independently of specific interiors. However, his furniture was intimately connected to his architecture. In the case of his built-in and freestanding cupboards, furniture became architecture by taking on the role of walls and partitions in addition to its primary function as storage. As we have seen, he even went so far as to incorporate structural elements of buildings into some of his furniture designs.

For Goldfinger, the primary objective of furniture and architecture was the same – to meet human needs. His storage designs did this more successfully than his chairs. One gets the impression that he was never entirely comfortable designing chairs, perhaps because it required an understanding of mass rather than space.

Top
1–3 Willow Road, Hampstead,
London.

Bottom left
Sideboard designed by
Goldfinger in 1935/6, dining
room, 2 Willow Road.

Bottom right
Entas chairs and table, dining
room, 2 Willow Road.

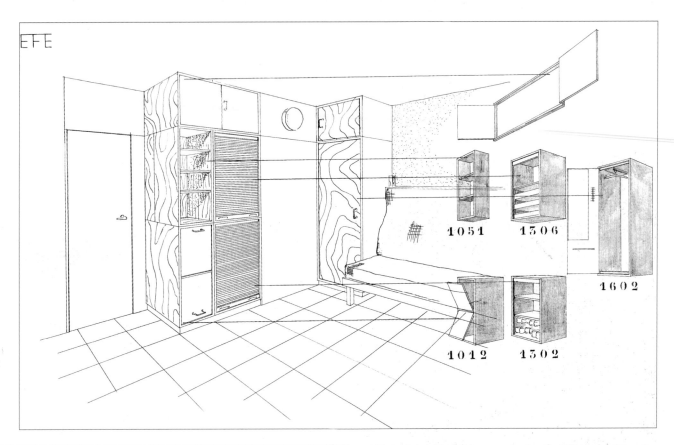

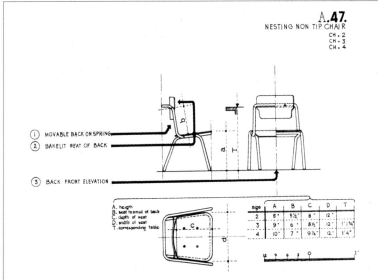

Above top
Design for Easiwork storage units, 1937.

Above bottom
Design for children's 'nesting' chair based on the Entas design, c 1934/5.

Primary sources:
Ernö Goldfinger Papers, Manuscripts and Archive Collection, British Architectural Library; RIBA
Ernö Goldfinger Drawings; Drawings Collection, British Architectural Library; RIBA
Willow Road Archive, 2 Willow Road; The National Trust.

Relevant public collections:
2 Willow Road, Hampstead, London.
V&A Museum, London
Design Museum, London
The Wolfsonian, Florida International University, Miami.

Although interested in ergonomics Goldfinger's attempts at ergonomic seating design tended to be technically lacking and awkward. He was far more adept at incorporating ergonomic principles into his designs for cupboards, desks, wardrobes etc, and this can be simply explained by the fact that designing storage was not so different from designing buildings. Both required the manipulation of space by means of horizontal and vertical elements to provide 'an ordered enclosure for human activities' or indeed for human possessions.[13]

The limitations of Goldfinger's chair designs are one of the main reasons why he failed to interest manufacturers in the production of his designs. One of the consequences of this lack of commercial success has been that his work as a furniture designer has been overshadowed by the architectural achievements of his later career. The lesser degree of interest that has been afforded to his furniture designs is to some extent wholly justified. His designs are not 'classics', and although progressive, Goldfinger did not lead the development of furniture design. However, in terms of understanding Goldfinger's career as an architect designer his designs are clearly important. The practice of designing furniture enabled him to explore his Modernist principles and develop his own style of expression in anticipation of architectural commissions. By diversifying in this way Goldfinger was also attempting what most architects associated with the Modern movement wanted to achieve, that is, the realisation of a new way of living appropriate to the 20th century. ⌀

Rebecca Milner studied art history at Warwick University and the Courtauld Institute of Art. She is Assistant Curator in the Furniture, Textiles and Fashion Department at the Victoria & Albert Museum, London. Her current area of research is British Modernism 1920–40.

Pure Form Only?

Observations on the Relationship Between Mies van der Rohe's Furniture and Buildings

For many years the classic black-and-white Modernist photos of Mies van der Rohe's interiors have portrayed him as 'a master of reduction and of cool elegance'. **Mateo Kries** reassesses this image by not only looking more closely at the material qualities of Mies's designs but also his aptitude for the drama and composition of interior spaces. He specifically draws our attention to the way that Mies used the technical innovation of steel-skeleton constructions to create interior design accents out of non-loadbearing materials. These partitions harmoniously mediated between the furniture and architecture, effectively linking the two.

In the short period between 1927 and 1931 Mies van der Rohe not only became one of the world's leading architects, but also designed some of the most significant furniture of the 20th century. In 1927 he created for the Weißenhof Siedlung in Stuttgart, of which he was the artistic director, the first ever cantilevered chair, and helped create a breakthrough in the use of tubular steel as a material for furniture. In 1929 Mies designed his legendary chair for the German Pavilion at the World Exhibition in Barcelona, as well as a chair and armchair for the Villa Tugendhat, one of the most important residential buildings of the 20th century. In 1931, at the Berlin Building Exhibition, Mies finally presented his previous designs as well as another classic, a sofa which simply consists of a horizontal surface and a cushion.

We know the interiors of the Barcelona Pavilion and the Villa Tugendhat from the black-and-white photographs from Mies van der Rohe's days. They show bare scenarios and austere room arrangements, totally in accordance with the idea of Neue Sachlichkeit. For a long time these arrangements corresponded to the image that the modern age had shaped out of Mies van der Rohe and his creative work. Mies was regarded as the master of reduction and as an architectonic ascetic.

The photographs by Thomas Ruff and Kay Fingerle, which are currently showing among the interiors of the Villa Tugendhat and the Barcelona Pavilion at the exhibition 'Mies in Berlin', give a totally different impression. They offer a new point of view of Mies's work as a designer of interiors in comparison to the historic black-and-white photographs. They show colourful, hyper-realistic scenarios where forms and materials seem to develop an independent existence, and room elements such as furniture, marble and wooden partition walls fit together to form completely different arrangements.

Of course, these photographs represent an artistic interpretation, but nevertheless make clear that the image of the architect of the century has changed. Mies was much more than only a master of reduction and of cool elegance. Working with materials, the perfection of the craft as well as technical innovations were more important to him than to follow exactly the aesthetic and social doctrines of the modern age. He strived for a dramaturgy of room sequences and for the staging of interiors, as he demonstrated in his most important works of his Berlin phase.

Mies used the technical innovation of steel-skeleton construction in order to implement non-bearing walls out of noble materials as interior design accents. So to speak, these walls became a link between furniture and architecture, whereas the piece of furniture – because of the disappearing of separate rooms – increasingly received the function of room structuring and architecture. The sculptures in Mies van der Rohe's interiors, mostly created by Georg Kolbe and Wilhelm Lehmbruck, also had the function of linking and structuring.

In contrast to many architects of the 1920s, Mies associated the right-angle only with architecture. For his steel furniture he preferred the organic line for ergonomic and technological reasons. He impressively demonstrated the appropriate aesthetic for tubular steel in the elegant curves of his tubular steel cantilever or the Barcelona chair.

Mies chose strap iron for many designs, such as the Barcelona chair and the Brno chair, a material which had not been used for furniture until then. Instead of the machine aesthetic of tubular steel Mies in this way

> Mies chose strap iron for many designs, such as the Barcelona Chair and the Brno Chair, a material which had not been used for furniture until then. Instead of the machine aesthetic of tubular steel Mies in this way achieved the impression of a bourgeois, elegant solidity.

achieved the impression of a bourgeois, elegant solidity. In the interiors of Barcelona and Brno the extensive profiles of the heavy strap iron, which is very difficult to handle, correspond with the extensive glass walls and the partition walls out of coloured glass or out of exquisitely patterned marble. The way Mies imagined the correspondence between furniture and space is revealed in the carefully composed historical photographs, in which the furniture is reflected in many different ways in the combination of transparent and translucent materials as well as surfaces covered with mirrors. A momentous fact, however, was that the photos concealed the harmony of colours of the furniture covers, which were made out of coloured silk as well as of the silk curtains and the marble wall.

One of the most dominant materials in Mies van der Rohe's rooms is a dark wood veneer, which he had already used for a group of wooden furniture for his own flat. Later on, this veneer is found in the semicircle partition wall of the Villa Tugendhat as well as in many more pieces of furniture that Mies had made for the furnishing of its private living rooms. Even through this means the architect still interpreted the room as a continuum – for example the veneer of the bridge table in the

Villa Tugendhat goes beyond all edges, so that the furniture's volume seems to be dissolving.

The construction details also reveal with what complexity Mies staged his own modern age. Since the large-scale production and the technology have made it possible, the frame of the Barcelona chair has been opulently welded. Its counterpart in architecture, the supporting pillar of the pavilion with its cross-shaped section, hides under its smooth chrome-plated cover a very complex interior. Mies gives other details particular emphasis, as for example the fixing of the armrest of the tubular steel cantilever to the frame, which is fastened simply with a clip. Mies van der Rohe's assistant Lilly Reich even applied for a registered design for the perfect edge of the wickerwork on the cantilever in terms of craftsmanship.

All this demonstrates that Mies was much more than only an advocate of steel and glass and simple reduction. Especially, the connection between furniture and buildings makes clear that Mies developed his ideas of modern architecture from his love of detail and the material as well as from his love of geometry and the craft, but not from theories. Mies was definitely uncompromising, but mainly when he followed his own ideas. Against this background it is understandable that Mies preferred well-to-do people as clients for his architecture, with whom he could fully realise his artistic ideas.

As a furniture designer Mies was a clever marketing strategist as well. He already had his designs patented and protected in the 1920s throughout Europe. Behind this strategy was Mies' adviser Anton Lorenz, who was also working together with Mart Stam and Marcel Breuer. With his consistent demand for patent protection Anton Lorenz flooded the emerging market for tubular steel furniture with a wave of legal proceedings, which partly continues until now. This paid off, because Mies could finance his costly lifestyle from the royalties, when the Nazis banned the new architecture in Germany. The royalties amounted to 1,175 Reichsmark in November 1936, when a worker earned approximately 180 Reichsmark per month.

When Mies emigrated to the USA in 1938, apart from a few sketches, the phase of his furniture designs was over. Maybe he wanted to fully concentrate on his commissions for buildings, which suddenly assumed enormous dimensions. Or maybe he realised that he had created icons with his brilliant designs in the 1920s, which he could not surpass anymore. ◊

Mateo Kries is director of the Vitra Design Museum in Berlin and curator of the international travelling exhibition 'Mies van der Rohe – furniture and buildings in Stuttgart, Barcelona, Brno'.

Translated from the German by Barbara Schmiedeknecht.

Max Bill

Simplicity and Ordinariness

Edwin Heathcote describes how the reductivist approach that is such a salient characteristic of contemporary Swiss architecture was foreshadowed by the work of the now little-known Modernist Max Bill. 'Monumentally unassuming', Bill's designs were pared down to 'the point of disappearance', stripped of any individual stylisations or signature flourishes. This is epitomised by his Ulm stool, which like his architecture, lacks the stylised geometry of fashionable Functionalism but is nonetheless deftly and economically conceived out of cheap materials. Ingenious in its ordinariness, the stool's design is perfectly honed for its use.

Today design has merged with fashion; function no longer means "the concurrence of all functions", i.e. design: the "function of design" ranges from promoting sales to pure gimmickry. We are right back at square one. Max Bill (1908–94), ranting against the subversion of modern design in 1988, was bemoaning the reappearance of a kind of design culture that never really went away. The history of the Modern movement is dominated by the quest for the 'functional aesthetic', in other words the appearance of machine production or the appearance of subservience to functionality. Bill stood apart from the mainstream of Modernism. Profoundly influential in graphic design, sculpture, art, product design and architecture, he remains curiously under-researched and relatively little-known outside his native Switzerland (although he has recently become a cult-figure among intellectual architects). This is almost certainly because of his uncompromising attachment to the ordinary and his complete rejection of the flashy motifs which characterised the Modernist and mid-century aesthetic. It is exactly this same thoughtful essentialism which makes his buildings and writings so pertinent to us today.

Bill was first turned on to architecture by seeing Le Corbusier's Pavilion de l'Esprit Nouveau at the Exposition Internationale des Arts Dècoratifs in Paris in 1925. He studied at the Bauhaus in Dessau between 1927 and 1929 and then returned to Switzerland where he became an internationally respected figure in both art and design. His Concrete Art inspired a whole movement in South America while he set the parameters for the Swiss style of graphics. He also built the school which became the breeding ground of the second phase of German Functionalism. So why does he remain obscure? The fundamental reason is that his designs are stripped down to the point of disappearance. Unlike the other great architect/designers of the Bauhaus – Gropius, Mies, Breuer et al – Bill's work remained monumentally unassuming. Philip Johnson once said that the reason Mies was great was that he was so easy to copy. Bill's self-effacing version of a Modernism of the mundane was unique and had no easy motifs to latch onto, unlike the stylised Functionalism of Mies, Breuer and Stam.

The key building of the machine aesthetic was Gropius's Bauhaus building in Dessau. This has become a 20th-century icon, instantly recognisable from the smallest detail. Bill designed and was the first head of the school that was the spiritual successor to the Bauhaus, the Hochschule für Gestaltung in Ulm (1950–55). Alison and Peter Smithson wrote:

> We think about the Ulm School of Art and Design – of its ease, of its ordinariness, that has a kind of understated lyricism which is full of potential and does not disturb the peace of the hillside on which it is situated.[1]

Yet, whereas the Bauhaus building has become an icon, like Breuer's chairs or Wilhelm Wagenfeld's lamp, Bill's building has remained a cult favourite at best.

Perhaps this is precisely because, like Bill's other work, it gives no easy aesthetic solutions; raw, cheap and lacking the geometrical plan rigour of Functionalism it has been stripped of anything that could be copied by a magpie architectural culture and therefore remains relatively unfamiliar. If Breuer's tubular chairs can be seen as the embodiment of Bauhaus principles, and one of the few Bauhaus-designed products to become truly commercially viable and successful, then it is one of Bill's pieces of furniture, the Ulm stool, which defines his contribution to design. The Ulm stool is possessed of the same reductivist characteristics as the building for which it was designed.

Pared down to the simplest possible U-section, the Ulm stool remains one of the most remarkable designs of the twentieth century, remarkable in that its very ordinariness, its lack of glamour and the cheapness of the beech from which it was made, the combination of its austerity, cheapness and availability seems to defy the cult of the collectible.

By the time the Hochschule für Gestaltung was completed in the harsh economic climate of post-war Germany, there was little money left for furniture. The idea behind the stool was that each student would carry his or her own seat from class to class to facilitate the most economic furnishing solution. The stool has a dual use, however. As the students were already burdened with books and papers, the stool could be turned upside down and carried by the dowel stretcher, the books carried on the underside of the seat. Pared down to the simplest possible U-section, the Ulm stool remains one of the most remarkable designs of the 20th century, remarkable in that its very ordinariness, its lack of glamour and the cheapness of the beech from which it was made, the combination of its austerity, cheapness and availability seems to defy the cult of the collectible.

For the same building, Bill also designed one of the most enduring pieces of door furniture, a remarkably simple curving handle which is just as self-effacing as the stool, its very neutrality assuring its longevity. The door handle is the consummate crossover between architecture and furniture, it is, after all, door furniture, and its form is among the most complete expositions of Bill's non-dogmatic approach to design. Most

of the Bauhaus designers, when it came to designing a door handle, created designs which looked machine made. Gropius's cylindrical barrel with a squared shaft is the best-known, Wagenfeld's design with an elegantly elongated grip and three-quarter circle shaft is a Functionalist icon. Bill's handle, however, is curving and ergonomic, a smoothed banana as opposed to a clinical machine-part. It is this sacrificing of the Functionalist aesthetic for the sake of a comfortable grip and an anonymous intervention which has made the handle among the most enduring designs (visitors to the Walsall Art Gallery, Britain's finest contemporary building, can see it there) but also the most influential.

In the curving handle can be seen the idea of what came to be known as 'Die Gute Form' (hard to translate, possibly 'good form', or 'the right form'). This phrase became a rallying cry in German design in the rough period after the Second World War. Bill organised a touring exhibition of that name in the first year of the Hochschule für Gestaltung. It was a brave exhibition, the suggestion of which was that the reconstruction of the bombed-out Germany must be carefully considered and carefully and thoughtfully designed from the smallest detail to the largest urban reconstruction. When the exhibition reached Cologne, a spark of genius touched its curation and the new, well-designed objects were placed among the ruins of the bombed-out city, the juxtaposition intended to suggest that the salvation of the nation, its future, lay in design, that from this chaos and destruction a better (ie designed) world should emerge. Bill wrote about 'striving towards the ideal condition wherein all forms, from the smallest object to a city, should also be conceived as 'the sum total of all functions in harmonious unison', becoming self-evident parts of our daily life. This condition could then be called culture – which is our aim.'

Indeed, some of Bill's best-known designs have embodied the reductivist Modernist aesthetic in a clearer fashion than any of his contemporaries. The watches and clocks he designed for German manufacturer Junghans are exemplary works of minimalism. Their faces are clear, severe and share the same readability and clarity as his graphic design.

Above
Ulm stool.

Right
Watches for Junghans, 1962.

In fact, all of those intimately involved with the practice or theory of architecture will be familiar with at least one of Bill's designs, and it is one which is worth looking at for a number of reasons.

We have already seen that Bill was inspired to take up architecture by the work of Corb. The two architects can, in some ways, be seen as the opposite poles of Modernism. Corb, like Bill was an artist. But he was in love with his own celebrity image. His constantly changing work, from the exquisite villas of the 1920s to the expressionistic indulgence of Ronchamp can all be seen as a quest for greatness. From the enthusiastic embodiment of the machine aesthetic to the passion for concrete shown in La Tourette or Chandigarh, Corb's work is a kind of sculpture, art made as proof of his genius. Bill on the other hand, despite being in charge of the Hochschule für Gestaltung was never a star, and, in all but architectural and academic circles, remains an enigma if known at all. His monk-like shaven head certainly never appeared on the cover of *Time* magazine like Corb's (or Wright's). While Corb scribbled murals on the walls of Eileen Gray's dream-like villa (against her wishes) and painted away in the nude, Bill's art was based on mathematics, on the Moebius band and on highly abstract ideas of infinity and continuity. Yet at one point, the paths of the two men crossed to produce a monumental, enormously influential and intimately familiar work.

On the shelves of every major architecture library, a certain set of books is always very visible: the stencil-type letters on the spines of the volumes of the *Oeuvre Complète* of Le

Corbusier and Pierre Jeanneret. One of these was written and designed by Bill. The design is simple and of great clarity, far less theatrical than Corb's headline-grabbing buildings which initially inspired him. Bill wanted to build but, in the period after he left the Bauhaus at Dessau (from 1928), he had few opportunities and instead made a living as a graphic designer. He wrote in 1930: 'I had decided not to erect any spectacular buildings, but rather to take pains to remain financially reasonable and not to incur any unnecessary expenditures. This moral principle inevitably led to an aesthetic of the useful that is denounced as exceptionally puritanical. This puritanism, for purely common sense reasons, always brought me back to the production of commercial art pieces, theoretically as well as practically'.[2]

His books on Robert Maillart (which identified the beauty of the truly functional aesthetic of the engineer)[3] and on *Modern Swiss Architecture*[4] remain exemplars of book design which many architects still seem to treat as definitive. It could be argued that the success of Koolhaas and Mau is a direct challenge to Bill's pragmatism and works because Bill's designs had already set the standard in clarity and progression which are still revered and which they have destroyed to great effect.

Bill's commercial art was also instrumental in bringing him into the realm of furniture design. In 1931 he was called in to design the logo for new Swiss

Bottom right
Catalogue for Wohnbedarf, Zurich, 1931. The brochure was designed by Max Bill, with distinct typography. The models are Bill and his wife and the furniture is also designed by Bill.

Bottom left
Advertisement by Max Bill for a Wohnbedarf exhibition, 1932.

furniture manufacturer Wohnbedarf. The commission became, in effect, a complete rebranding and Bill was called on to design furniture and advertising – indeed, he and his wife, Binia (a photographer who often worked with her husband) regularly appeared in the company's ads, lounging on recliners, reading or otherwise inhabiting the Modernist domestic habitat.

Wohnbedarf was a fascinating and pioneering Modernist concern. Its founders were Sigfried Giedion, Werner Moser and Rudolf Graber. Marcel Breuer was called in to design its wonderful (and still extant) stripped-down Zurich headquarters. Wohnbedarf's staple products were a series of bentwood chairs designed by Swiss architect Moser, who knew Bill from the Bauhaus. Although clearly influenced by Thonet chairs, Moser's designs had been reduced to the bare bones – a rush seat, and curving rear legs rising to support a single looping backrest. It had become a café and restaurant staple. The firm was also selling bentwood furniture designs by Alvar Aalto before he set up Artek in 1935. Bill designed the company's corporate image, the logo (a version of which is still in use today), its publicity, stationery and invitations. He also went on to design a number of pieces of furniture for the company, including a three-legged chair, a stackable chair and a simple three-legged coffee table.

A complete departure from the rigour of the Ulm stool, these pieces featured what could best be described as plectrum shapes. Very much a part of the 'Gute Form' aesthetic, these were more forgiving shapes, more associated with comfort, but there was a lack of the self-conscious ergonomic engineering aesthetic (which had by now replaced the Functionalist/ machine-made aesthetic as the avant-garde of modernism) that characterised the work of many of Bill's contemporaries (Eames, Jacobsen et al). On the other hand, the plectrum shape does date the piece, a precursor of the kidney shapes which would proliferate in a few years to dominate apple-pie suburban sitting rooms.

Both the coffee table and the chair featured three legs. The device suited the unusual (shield/plectrum) shape of the seat/surface. It also made it incredibly dangerous to lazily lean back on the chair's rear leg. This was of no use in schools and, perhaps in part, the reason for the recent discontinuation of the line. The device was, however, taken up again by Philippe Starck (perhaps the designer at the furthest possible opposite end of the spectrum to Bill) for his chairs for the Café Costes in Paris which, unlike Bill's far more elegant models, remain in production (though the Café Costes itself disappeared long ago, presumably due to people leaning back on their chairs!). All of Bill's furniture designs, with the exception of the Ulm stool which has recently been taken up by Vitra in a far-sighted and shrewd move, have been discontinued.

A complete departure from the rigour of the Ulm stool, these pieces featured what could best be described as plectrum shapes. Very much a part of the 'Gute Form' aesthetic, these were more forgiving shapes, more associated with comfort, but there was a lack of the self-conscious ergonomic engineering aesthetic that characterised the work of many of Bill's contemporaries.

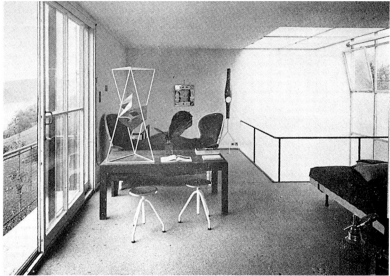

Opposite top
Curved triangular table,
1949–50.

Opposite middle
Three legged chair, 1950.

Above top
View from the garden of Max
Bill's House, Zurich, 1932–33.

Above middle
Interior of Max Bill's House,
Zurich, 1932–33.

Footnotes
1. Von Moos, Stanislaus,
Minimal Tradition, Swiss
Federal Office of Culture
(Zurich), 1996, p 38.
2. Ibid, p 17,
3. Max Bill, *Robert Maillart*,
Verlag fur Architektur (Zurich),
1949.
4. Max Bill, *Modern Swiss
Architecture*, Verlag Karl
Werner (Basel), 1942.
5. Claude Lichtenstein and
Thomas Schregenberger (eds)
*As Found: the Discovery of
the Ordinary*, Lars Muller
Publishers (Zurich), 2001.

This puritanism of his design has also seen Bill grouped together with a generation of post-war British cultural figures who had become used to the rigour of rationing and the idea of utility. A recent book, *As Found: the Discovery of the Ordinary* (edited by Claude Lichtenstein and Thomas Schregenberger)[5] attempts to weave a link between such seemingly unconnected phenomena as Kitchen Sink Drama, New Brutalism, gritty English film-making and the stripped-down architectural aesthetic of Bill which then inspired the Smithsons, Colin St John Wilson and others in Britain.

Although not necessarily immediately apparent, there does seem to be a series of interesting links. British design at the same time was dominated by figures who had been influenced by the self-deprecating ideas of 'Gute Form' and industrial designers from the Bauhaus tradition – Wagenfeld, Braun-Feldweg, Guhl, Bill (and later Hans Gugelot and Dieter Rams), while the public mood was caught between the grim reality of rationing and a fantasy world of disposable pop culture coming

from the USA, visible in magazines and films but utterly intangible.

The one house Bill built between the wars, including his own studio, is an exemplar of the self-deprecation of his design, and presaged a number of new developments in Modernism, some of which are only now emerging. The house's pitched roof for instance was profoundly un-Bauhaus, while the chimney flue supported on a Heath Robinson system of struts and braces is odd yet leaves the spaces inside pure and clean. The windows are enormous in the case of the studios, merely very large in the domestic spaces. The light fittings are rudimentary, bulbs sticking out of the wall using the most basic sockets, and the radiators are used as space modulators rather than just adjuncts to the walls. Where possible doors and cabinets slide open (there are similarities here with Goldfinger's stripped-down but exquisite built-in fittings) and the furniture (most of it designed by Bill himself before he became known as a product designer) is utterly basic, completely unselfconscious and purely functional, now looking, frankly, extremely hip. Similar basic wall and ceiling sockets and naked bulbs are to be seen in the work of a number of young London architects.

The recent remarkable rise of Swiss architecture is also, perhaps, the legacy of Max Bill. Herzog & De Meuron, Gigon & Guyer, Peter Märkli, Diener & Diener and others have revived an appreciation of the simple and the restrained over the showy and expressive for which Bill was known, although they have tended to tinge it with a more knowing and deliberate minimalism. Bill was the man who made expo and exhibition stands look like industrial sheds. And ordinary ones at that. His revelling in the everyday language of industrial materials (truly off the shelf not, Bauhaus-like, made to look industrial) and of edge-of-city constructions (the true 20th-century contribution to architecture) now seems incredibly modern. His influence is also clear in the work of a generation of British architects who grew up with the dominant, overpowering strains of Po-Mo, High-Tech and designer minimal and have found Bill an unassuming and sympathetic antidote to the unappealing brashness of 1980s extremes. Caruso St John, Sergison Bates, David Adjaye and 6a all obviously draw inspiration from the pared-down but not over-refined aesthetic sensibility of Bill's work.

In furniture, Bill's legacy is less clear. Most of his designs have been taken out of production in recent years, just as interest in him is reviving. Watches, door handles and the Ulm stool are still selling but it is precisely his anti-style approach that has made him hard to market; his eschewal of the star-architect role during his life has mitigated against his posthumous superstardom. Instead he remains on the margins and boundaries, his work half-remembered, its lesson the profound value of the simple and the ordinary. ⌀

Oxford's 'Best Motel'
The Dining Room at
St Catherine's College, Oxford

For Arne Jacobsen, St Catherine's College, Oxford, was a unique opportunity
for total design. Responsible for the buildings, interior space and furniture,
Jacobsen also played a part in the college's landscaping. **Sarah Jackson** describes
how everything was produced with such acute attention to detail and exquisite
workmanship that ordinary materials were elevated to precious stones. Nowhere
is this more apparent than in the dining room, which epitomises Jacobsen's seamless
approach to architectural structure, detailing and individual items of furniture.

One iconic image of the 1960s – the naked Christine Keeler astride a veneered ply chair – could be said to define the political moment; today it says as much about Arne Jacobsen. Unlike most architect-designed furniture, Jacobsen's work has managed to bridge the gap between popular and high culture. This is for a number of reasons; his pieces are humane and domestic, both in scale and materials (there is little of the Bauhaus leather and chrome, with the obvious masculine, office associations) and the chairs are all commercially produced, allowing price and quality to be optimised. But perhaps more important, are the anthropomorphised forms and names; Ant, Tongue, Egg, Swan – cheeky, friendly and warm. The Keeler chair is in fact a copy of Jacobsen's series 7 chair, the chair with the dubious accolade of being 'the most copied stacking chair in the world'.[1] It is copied because it is so good.

Although Jacobsen is best known for his furniture, his true skills were architectural. He designed furniture for specific building projects, and their commercial viability was only realised once the project was complete. Jacobsen had a long and mutually beneficial relationship with the Danish furniture manufacturer Fritz Hansen, which still makes and markets his pieces today.

St Catherine's College, Oxford (1960–64) is arguably one of Jacobsen's finest works,[2] and certainly his favourite.[3] As the college was new, it was conceived as a complete whole; Jacobsen designed everything from the landscape and buildings, down to the furniture and cutlery. St Catherine's is set down on a rectangular podium, with two wings of study bedrooms on the long sides, and three major communal buildings – dining hall, library and lecture hall – in the centre. The buildings are unified by a rigorously applied module, the repeated use of prefabricated elements and the consistency of materials (concrete, brick and glass) throughout. All is seemingly simple, but everything is so resolved, with an acute attention to detail and such exquisite workmanship that these ordinary materials are elevated to precious stones. Pevsner rightly called it 'perfect',[4] and Banham, in a characteristic Lolita-ish tone called it Oxford's 'best motel'.[5]

The dining hall is the largest (it seats around 350 people) and surely the most monastic in Oxford. Green slate floor, brick walls and the volume ordered by pairs of cruciform concrete columns, it is richly severe. These precast columns, set at the 'regulation' 3.2-metre module, support 1.5-metre-deep beams, which in turn support the roof and light beams above; the quality of this concrete is enviably luscious – the sections are so thin, so deep, so long, and the material smooth and silken. The hall is classically axial, but despite the ceremonial focus of the dais, all interest is on the long side walls. Here, the ethereal cantilevered roof beams stretch sideways and crash outside, the brick shrinks to suit and the junction is taken by glass. The short end wall is more subdued, but equally considered. There is no glass – it is all brick – but the brick is segmented into panels, each one slightly angled as if pleated to form a slight curve; part acoustic, part decoration, it is a solemn backdrop for the dais at the end of the room.

There is no misunderstanding about the top table and chairs. The chairs are tall, some thirty in number, throne-like and superior; those who sit are in power. Face on, the chairs appear almost square but at just the slightest angle they show a double spine-like curve. They are constructed out of a single oak-veneered plywood piece; the originals had four bent plywood legs which fixed to the underside, but as these proved to be unstable they were replaced by aluminium pedestals. The central chair, which is used by the College Master, is slightly taller, and upholstered in leather. Individually the chairs have great sculptural presence, but collectively they form a room of their own; at formal meals the Fellows both belong to the hall and are in their own private dining room. Not surprisingly the

Opposite top left
The precast concrete columns
and beams of the dining room:
the quality of this concrete is
enviably luscious – the
sections are so thin, so deep,
so long, and the material
smooth and silken.

Opposite top right
Dining room in St Catherine's
College. The tables and
benches can accommodate
some 320 students.

Opposite bottom
Column to beam junction at
the crenellated side wall.

Above left
The same chairs are also used
in a smaller private Fellows'
dining room.

Above right
Detail of the short segmented
end brick wall of the dining
room.

Below left
The Fellows' chairs and
central chair used by the
College Master.

Below middle
Upholstered in leather, the
College Master's chair is
slightly taller than those of the
Fellows. Note the original (but
modified) bent plywood legs.

Below right
End view of students' bench,
with similar joint detail to the
column beam junction.

Footnotes
1. David Nicholls, 'The
information', The Independent,
2 March 2002, p 10.
2. The new monograph,
published to coincide with his
centenary year, is an excellent
overview of Jacobsen. Carslen
Thau and Kjeld Vindum,
Jacobsen, Danish Architectural
Press, 2001.
3. Margaret and Derek Davies,
Creating St Catherine's
College, St Catherine's College
(Oxford), 1997, p 101.
4. J Sherwood and N Pevsner,
Buildings of England: Oxford,
Penguin (London), 1974.
5. Reyner Banham, 'St
Catherine's College, Oxford',
Architectural Review, vol 136,
September 1964.

chairs are unusual to sit in – both aloof throne
and cosy settle. They are relatively comfortable,
but actually quite awkward, the high back feels
like a large spindly blinkers and it blocks you
from your neighbour when you twist.

This was one of the last chairs that Jacobsen
designed, and it can be seen as a culmination of
his earlier organic forms and later technological
developments – a slice of a fixed bench from
Sollerod City Hall (1934) combined with his
1950s bent plywood chairs (Ant, Tongue, series
7). Fritz Hansen still produces an evolved
version of the St Catherine's chair, called the
Oxford series; design changes have been made
to make an otherwise very specific chair more
acceptable to the general market. The Oxford
chairs are upholstered in leather, have
aluminium pedestal legs (with or without
castors), are available in four back heights, and
with the option of arms. They are both elegant
and comfortable, and wholly appropriate for
corporate meeting rooms and restaurants, but
they are not really the same chair. The subtle
fine line and the continuity of material (plywood
body to leg) is gone, and with that the chair
loses its power.

The main body of the hall is taken up by ten
long tables, each with three benches per side,
enough to seat over three hundred students.
They are placed parallel to the long wall,
perpendicular to the top table. The benches
(which were made by the English firm of Gordon
Russell and Company) at first seem rather

simple – oak continuous tops supported by three square
framed legs. But the third element, a spine frame
running underneath the seat bracing the three legs
together, provides a level of detail that makes these
benches far from ordinary. The separation of elements
mimics that of the beams and roof, and the joint
between the leg and spine frame is visually identical
to the main column / beam junction – interlocking,
cruciformed and extremely considered.

With these two pieces, the high chair and the bench,
Jacobsen has shown how the richness implicit in St
Catherine's elevates it from what could easily have been
a rigid and stifling design. The grand statement chairs,
with their back wall, face into the introverted hall, both
quiver, their subtle curves emphasised by the hard
surfaces that surround. The benches, however, achieve
a level of depth equivalent to the college as a whole.
By using the same joint detail, Jacobsen both raised
the status of the humblest of items, the student bench,
to that of the accepted mighty, the beams and columns,
and also shows us the timber root of this trabeated
construction. And, by virtue of their location, the
benches, or more accurately the students, can dream
through the crenellated glass slots, through to the
world outside.

St Catherine's is at first glance an essay in concrete,
brick and stone, but it is in effect an archaic timber
temple. Order and rigour in architectural form has
allowed freedom of movement and thought. The
furniture reminds us of that. ◬

Sarah Jackson is an architect and architectural
historian. She works in practice, teaches and writes.

American Moderns
Eero Saarinen
and his Circle

Eero Saarinen's furniture has become the first choice for cutting-edge interiors, with his designs cropping up in hip restaurants, office spaces and residential projects. **Jayne Merkel** gives the background to this current revival of interest in the Expressionist forms of Saarinen's moulded fibreglass furniture by tracing the emergence of his work back to the particular convergence of a group of talents from Cranbrook, which included Charles Eames and Florence Knoll, as well as Saarinen and his famous father.

You know you're getting old when the 'far out' furniture of your youth starts showing up in antique shops. But when Eero Saarinen's chairs appear in the Diller+Scofidio superchic Brasserie at the Seagram Building (in soft white leather, no less), you think: perhaps my time has come.

Saarinen's certainly has. *Interiors* magazine's Designer of the Year, Yabu Pushelberg of Toronto, used Saarinen chairs in the sensational (if not exactly elegant) new Times Square W Hotel restaurant. And AJS Designs took some out of one of Hungry Man's filmsets to use in the production company's reception space.

After years of relative obscurity, Eero Saarinen is back (though a row of his almost-classic Tulip chairs has always been in the ladies lounge at Philip Johnson's Four Seasons Seagram Building restaurant). Last spring, crowds filled the chambers of New York City's Landmarks Preservation Commission to protest against a plan to turn Saarinen's sweeping TWA Terminal at Kennedy Airport into a conference centre; architects the world over sent the preservationists letters of support.

Clearly, some of the revived interest grows out of the current fascination with Expressionistic form, but that doesn't quite explain the popularity of the furniture, which is much broader based – and surprising in a country that still hasn't fully accepted modern design.

Conservatism was even more entrenched when Eero Saarinen's father Eliel came to the United States from Finland in 1923, met the newspaper heir George Booth, and helped him found an artists' colony on the Booth family estate in Bloomfield Hills, Michigan, outside Detroit. But unlike Hvitträsk, the compound of houses with

studios that Eliel and his young partners at Gesellius, Lindgren and Saarinen, had built on a lake outside Helsinki in 1902, Cranbrook (as the American community came to be called) contained institutions – girls' and boys' schools, an art academy, museums and libraries as well as homes for resident artists. The elder Saarinen designed all the buildings and furnishings and directed the Cranbrook Academy of Art, where he influenced the first generation of American moderns.

Eero worked with him and also taught at Cranbrook for a while, though he studied elsewhere (sculpture at the Academie de la Grande Chaumière in Paris, 1929–30, and architecture at Yale University, 1931–34).[1] During his school years, he collaborated with his father on the Kingswood School for Girls, designing its Aaltoesque birch chairs with curved backs and International Style tubular steel seating for the auditorium. He then spent two years travelling and working in Finland with Karl Eklund. During that time saw not only Aalto's latest work but that of the European avant-garde.

Back at Cranbrook, he met Charles Eames and was reacquainted with Florence Schust (Knoll), who had been practically adopted by his parents after hers died when she was a student at Kingswood. She went to Finland with the Saarinens every summer. 'Shu' took classes in the Cranbrook Academy of Art graduate school before she even went to college, first at Columbia University in New York, then at the Architectural Association in London, and finally at the Illinois Institute of Architecture in Chicago under Mies van der Rohe. Also at Cranbrook in the late 1930s were the sculptor Harry Bertoia, the city planner Edmund Bacon, architects Ralph Rapson and Harry Weese, and designers Benjamin Baldwin, Ray Kaiser (who became Eames's wife and partner), Eero's sister, Pipsan Saarinen Swanson, and Eero's first wife, Lily Swann, who studied ceramics.

CONVERSATION

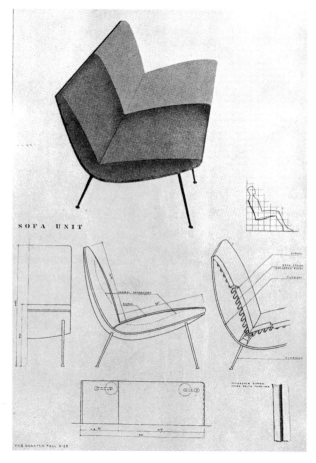

SOFA UNIT

Top left, right and bottom 'Organic Design' chairs. A series of chairs and settees designed by Eero Saarinen and Charles Eames with the help of other members of the Cranbrook community won first prize in the Seating for a Living Room category of the Museum of Modern Art's 'Organic Design in Home Furnishings' competition of 1940. An armchair was made of plaster on wire mesh. The plaster shell was fractured to conform to the human body and reset in a light crate of strips of masonite. Next, a cast iron mould was made from the crate, and the wood shell of the final chair was glued up in the mould. Shells were trimmed and fitted with rubber. Although the designers originally envisioned aluminium legs, wooden ones were substituted in production because of the difficulty of procuring the intended rubber weld joint.

It is not surprising that Florence Knoll thought, 'The design world is very small, and in those days (the 1940s), everyone knew everyone else'.[2] And it was not just a matter of knowing one another. They shared an attitude toward design that came directly from Eliel Saarinen. 'My father', Eero once said, 'saw architecture as everything from city planning to the ash tray on a living room table'.[3]

That attitude – that everything is architecture, and all scales are intertwined – was the foundation for their work. Modern furniture was essential in a modern building. If it didn't exist, you had to design it.

It was an uphill battle in America, especially when Eliel arrived. Cranbrook gave him an opportunity to design everything from a campus plan to door knobs. But the only other interiors he was asked to do in the late 1920s and early 1930s were for the Hudnut Building in New York and two exhibitions that the Metropolitan Museum of Art put on in 'a concerted effort [by] American designers, museums, department stores, and manufacturers to foster modern design in this country' after the Exposition Internationale des Arts Décoratifs and Industriels Modernes in Paris of 1925.[4] The idea was to encourage designs for mass production, but most of the furniture on display, including Eliel's (which had elaborate inlay), required too much craftsmanship to be economical. Like the work in the French Exposition, it was still considerably more conservative than that designed at the Bauhaus.

The same could not be said for the prize-winning chairs, sectional sofas, modular storage units and tables that Eero Saarinen and Charles Eames designed together for the 'Organic Design in Home Furnishings Competition' at the Museum of Modern Art in 1940 (with help from Ray Eames, Don Albinson, and Harry Bertoia).[5] Their starkly geometric mahogany-veneer chests were a domesticated version of the modular metal furniture Marcel Breuer produced at the Bauhaus, and their double-curved chairs belong to the worlds of Aalto's bent plywood chairs, Surrealist sculpture, and imminent Abstract Expressionism. These pieces were not only designed to be mass produced; they were actually manufactured (by the Haskelite manufacturing corporation and the Heywood-Wakefield Company).[6] It was only because of the onset of the Second World War that the effort came to naught. In addition, these pieces influenced furniture later created by both Eero and Eames – and Florence Knoll. But it still took a museum intent on promoting modern design to instigate them.[7]

Knoll explained in her memoirs how hard it was to create modern furniture for the market at the time.[8] When she moved to New York and was working for Harrison & Abramovitz, she met the son of a family of German furniture manufacturers, Hans Knoll, who was starting a new business and needed someone to create modern interiors to show his chairs. She started moonlighting for him, quit her day job, and began collaborating with him as an interior space planner and designer. In 1943 she also became his wife.

'The beginnings were very tough', she recalled. 'Not only was it difficult to get contemporary work, but it was extremely difficult to get the furniture produced once we had the client and the job. Fabrics were difficult. Even the glues were inferior. The only material available at the

Above
'Organic Design' modular storage units. Saarinen and Eames's wood chests, shelves and benches, which could be placed on legs, won first prize in the MoMA's Other Furniture for a Living Room category. The flexible and practical components were domesticated with Honduras mahogany veneer and the simple cubic indentations that functioned as pulls. Yet the system carried the principle of standardisation further than any produced in the United States. Units were based on an 18-inch module and could be set on a standard base with 13-inch legs which multiplied potential uses, made them easier to clean under, and to place against a wall.

time was wood. Everything was on a wartime basis.'[9]

Luckily, Eero responded to the challenge. He had given up his teaching post at Cranbrook in 1942 to concentrate on practice, and worked for the Office of Strategic Services in Washington DC, during the war. Knoll saw him: 'constantly in those days. He was like a brother, and since we had a lot of time then, we talked a lot. One thing led to another in the development of his furniture. His first piece was laminated wood because we weren't able to get other materials. It was the only laminated chair he did'. The Aaltoesque Grasshopper chair (of 1943) with its bent wood arms 'was a perfectly nice chair, but it wasn't one of the great successes'.[10]

Then he began working on molted fibreglass furniture, which is when his 'breakthrough' came.[11]

His plan was to do a whole series of fibreglass chairs. I said, 'Why not take the bull by the horns and do the big one first?' and that's what happened.... Eero developed the womb chair...at my specific request because I was sick and tired of structured chairs which held you in one position. I wanted a chair which was like a basket full of pillows, something I could curl up in. Eero did the prototype, using his own office in Bloomfield Hills as the research lab.

He asked everyone who came into the office to try it out. Unlike many architects, including some who called themselves 'Functionalists', he was concerned with the chair's comfort – not just the role it would play in the design of a room. He even considered how people would look sitting in it.[12]

When Eero and Charles Eames worked on their submissions to the Museum of Modern Art competition, Eero developed the ideas and it was Eames who figured out how to build them.[13] But when Eero was creating the chairs for Knoll, he 'worked with the moulds himself', Knoll recalled, and helped her find someone to build it.

We finally found a shipbuilder, named Winter, in New Jersey who was working in fibreglass. Eero and I went out there to beg him to make us some models. He was very sceptical. I guess because we were so young and so enthusiastic and because we just begged him so much, he finally gave in and worked with us. We had lots of problems and failures before we finally got a chair that would work.

He even helped her patent it. 'Eero and I sat with a tough patent lawyer for an entire afternoon.... We did get patents, which is remarkable, and it's the only chair I know of that has a patent. Oddly enough, the patent was based on cutting a hole and a few other things'. (The distinctive hole may also have been the result of the cone moulding process, as R. Craig Miller has contended.[14] Or the moulding process may have been what was patentable. There had been a hole in the seat of one of the chairs that Eames and Saarinen had designed together five years earlier for the Museum of Modern Art competition as well.) In any event, the adventure that led to the breakthrough chairs began, not on the playing fields of Eton, but in the studios of Cranbrook.

Eames, after whom Eero later named a son, said that though Eero's buildings look very different from one another, 'the thing that they did have in common was the fact that, to a remarkable degree, each building turned out to be a model of the problem. His furniture was similar to that'.[15]

Top
A Reception Area, General Motors Technical Center, c 1950.

Bottom
The Ultimate Pedestal Table for the House in Columbus, Indiana, 1953–57. Not only the legs and the top of this table, made specifically for the house, are all-in-one. There is no need for a vase or centrepiece either. A recessed basin in the middle enables flowers to float in the centre; a bubbling fountain provides additional effects.

Opposite top
Living Room 'Lounge Pit' in House in Columbus, Indiana, 1953–57. This grandfather of 'the conversation pit' that became all the rage in the 1960s was simply a recessed square in an open-plan pavilion house. Upholstered with sumptuous fabrics designed by Alexander Girard, the colour scheme changed with the four seasons, like that at Philip Johnson's only slightly later restaurant in the Seagram Building, which was named for that effect. A small open staircase steps down to the seating area which invites sprawling, curling up, and various ways of getting comfortable, while encouraging guests to partake in a single conversation as they might at a dinner table.

Opposite bottom
'Eero Saarinen as Furniture Designer', *Architectural Design*, October 1957. In the same year as Saarinen completed the House in Columbus, Indiana, Saarinen's furniture from Knoll's showrooms in New York was featured in *ᴀᴅ*.

Earo Saarinen as furniture designer

Niels Diffrient, who worked for Eero as a model maker when the chairs were being designed, explained: 'He came at a solution by process of elimination. He did a thousand solutions for any one design. You got what you got by throwing away everything that wasn't as good – but you tried everything. I had thought it was going to be a simple job of doing a chair with him for a month or two, but it was a year's effort'.[16]

Diffrient remembered Eero as 'very sombre and solid', except when 'Charlie [Eames] was around, he was more bubbly'. He was also impressed with Eero's affect on the Knolls: 'One day Hans and Shu Knoll turned up. Hans with a camel's hair coat draped over his shoulder, his blond Aryan good looks and tan in the middle of winter, sauntering in.... It was the first time I had ever seen people who exuded a sense of the world'. But Shu was part of the family: 'What I didn't appreciate was that Eero had an inside track with Knoll. Whatever he produced is what they did'.[17]

Eero, Shu and Charles had all absorbed Eliel Saarinen's sense of the whole:

Perhaps the most important thing I learned from my father was that in any design problem one should seek the solution in terms of the next largest thing. If the problem is an ashtray, then the way it relates to the table will influence its design. If the problem is a chair, then its solution must be found in the way it relates to the room.[18]

Eero's pedestal chairs take the form they do because 'the undercarriage of chairs and tables in a typical interior makes an ugly confusing, unrestful world. I wanted to clear up the slum of legs. I wanted to make the chair all one thing again'.[19]

Charles and Ray Eames, who moved to the West Coast in 1941, developed a design business of their own and went on to work with Knoll's main competitor, the Herman Miller Furniture Company in Michigan. But Knoll really didn't have much competition. Shu's Planning Unit offered interior design services unlike those available from any other manufacturer of the time. When she found that components were needed that did not exist in the line, she designed them herself. Now many of her simple, geometric, well-detailed 'background' pieces are classics in their own rights. She commissioned designs or bought the rights to existing ones from Harry Bertoia, Mies van der Rohe, Isamu Noguchi, Hans Bellman, Franco Albini, Joseph Frank, Pierre Jeanneret, Ilmari Tapiovarra and Mart Stam's version of Marcel Breuer's tubular steel armchair. But she eschewed homey Scandinavian and Expressionistic French and Italian designs, emphasising classics and keeping models in the catalogue for years. The firm developed a line of textiles. After the Second World War, Hans opened branches across the US and in 18 foreign countries.

One of Knoll's first big jobs came from Eero, who took over Saarinen and Saarinen's commission to design the General Motors Technical Center, a complex on 900 acres

Top left
'Number 72' side chairs in AJS
Design's Hungry Man's
kitchen–dining area.

Top right
Saarinen's womb chairs were
reupholstered by AJS Designs
for the reception area of the
offices of Hungry Man.

Bottom
AJS Designs made Saarinen's
pedestal table the centrepiece
for the Langer Residence, a
small apartment in New York's
West Village.

Footnotes
1. *Design in America, The
Cranbrook Vision 1935–50*,
Abrams (New York), 1983,
p 273.
2. Florence Schust Knoll,
typed, undated memoirs in
Knoll Associates archives.
3. Eero Saarinen in an address
at the Schöner Wohnen

Congress, Munich, 24 October 1960, in the Saarinen Archive at Yale University, reprinted in *Design in America*, op cit, pp 112–13.

4. Ibid, p 99.

5. Ibid, p 307, note 96.

6. Eliot F Noyes, *Organic Design in Home Furnishings*, Museum of Modern Art (New York), 1941, p 13.

7. Ibid, p 4. Noyes wrote in the introduction, 'The purpose of the contest was to discover good designers and engage them in the task of creating a better environment for today's living. Twelve important stores in major cities throughout the United States sponsored the competition and offered contracts with manufacturers as prizes to the winners.

8. Florence Knoll in the notes in the Knoll Archives.

9. Ibid.

10. Ibid.

11. Eric Larrabee and Massimo Vignelli, *Knoll Design*, Abrams (New York), 1981, p 56.

12. Marian Page, *Furniture Designed by Architects*, Whintney Library of Design, Watson-Guptill (New York), 1980, p 209.

13. *Design in America*, op cit, p 307, note 96. For his essay 'Interior design and furniture' (pp 91–144), R Craig Miller interviewed Buford Pickens on 18 November 1981 who told him that Eames went to Grand Rapids to study the manufacture of bent plywood theatre seating, and that Ralph Rapson, who was at Cranbrook when the submissions were designed, told him in an interview on 1 May 1982 that Saarinen developed ideas about chair forms but that it was Eames who took an interest in construction techniques.

14. Ibid, p 310, note 146. Miller interviewed Florence Knoll Bassett on 1 February 1982: 'Mrs Bassett noted that the chair had a hole in the back due to the cone moulding process and that the shell had to be completely upholstered due to the rough finish of the fibreglass. The shells were made by the Winner (sic) Manufacturing Company, Trenton, New Jersey, of fibres bonded with Paraplex P-43 resin', and cites 'Chemistry builds a chair', Rohn & Hass Reporter, Nov–Dec 19561, pp 2–4 as a source.

15. *Knoll Design*, op cit, p 50.

16. Ibid, p 56.

17. Ibid.

18. Ibid, p 57.

19. Ibid.

20. *Knoll Design*, op cit, p 56.

21. *Robert AM Stern, Thomas Mellins, David Fishman, New York 1960*, Monacelli Press (New York), 1995,

in Warren, Michigan even before his father died in 1950. The buildings that Eliel had envisioned as streamlined Art Moderne structures surrounding a lake became more geometric and industrial in crisp metal and glass arranged in an asymmetrical plan that resembled that at Mies's Illinois Institute of Technology. But in Eero's hands, the International Style vocabulary was jazzier and more American.

> In Eero's hands, the International Style vocabulary was jazzier and more American. Enormous structures spread way out over the land on the scale of the motor car. Long bands of metal contrasted with dark glass, set off by a smaller intense-red rectangular building.

Enormous structures spread way out over the land on the scale of the motor car. Long bands of metal contrasted with dark glass, set off by a smaller intense-red rectangular building, the reflective steel hemisphere of the 'styling dome' and a shiny metal oval water tower hovering 120 feet over the lake on three tubular legs. The long walls of the buildings were made of thin prefabricated porcelain-faced interior and exterior sandwich panels sealed with new neoprene gaskets. Inside, the 'Number 71' chairs with holes in the seats that Eero had designed for Knoll, a new cubic armchair, and geometric furnishings by Florence Knoll were used throughout the 25 buildings of the $100 million complex and arranged in rectangular groupings like those in the industrial campus plan. The short end walls were covered with glazed bricks in primary colours.

Architecture, interior design and furniture came together even more completely in a house for the industrialist and architectural patron of Columbus, Indiana, of 1953–57, on which Saarinen worked with the designer Alexander Girard and the landscape architect Daniel Urban Kiley. This glass- and slate-walled pavilion, surrounded by a grid of trees, had a pinwheel plan of spaces that flowed into one

another in the centre. The dining room table was an elegant, enlarged version of the pedestal table with a recessed basin in the centre for floating flowers and a fountain. And the living room most completely expressed the idea that 'a room is like a piece of art: it is just one idea'.[20] Here, Saarinen got rid of the 'slum of legs' by burying the seating area and putting cushions around its edges to form a gigantic square couch. It became the inspiration of the 'conversation pits' that New York architects Paul Rudolph, Der Scutt and even Robert AM Stern built into their own apartments in the 1960s.[21] When Stern showed his in a lecture a few years ago, the audience erupted in giggles. But in a year or two, who knows, maybe even they will rise (or sink) again.

Afterword

Knoll International has remained the premier contract furniture company in the US though Hans Knoll died in a car accident while in Cuba to open a branch there in 1955. Florence Knoll carried on for another decade but eventually remarried (becoming Florence Knoll Bassett) and moved to Florida. Eero Saarinen died of a brain tumour in 1961. Charles Eames, who lived until 1978 in Los Angeles, designing a little bit of everything in partnership with his wife Ray, erected a pavilion for the New York World's Fair of 1964 based on a design he had developed with Saarinen years earlier. And at Cranbrook, the tradition of ambitious architecture has continued with recent buildings and additions by Steven Holl, Tod Williams, Billie Tsie and Associates, the Office of Peter Rose, and Rafael Moneo. But there has never been quite the same convergence of major talents in residence there, or a similar collection of American designers drawing together on a blank slate as there was when Eero Saarinen, Charles Eames, Florence Schust and their contemporaries set the stages people are walking on today. Δ

Jayne Merkel is a contributing editor to *Architectural Design* who first considered Eero Saarinen's furniture when she wrote a master's thesis on 'Eliel Saarinen at Cranbrook' under Henry Russell Hitchcock and Leonard Eaton. A former editor of *Oculus* magazine in New York, she is now at work on a monograph on Eero Saarinen for Phaidon Press.

Look at me
Look at me

As **Neil Cummings** points out, 'sitting seems one of the uses we least require of the chair'. Here he looks at the relatively recent phenomenon of 'furniturization', which is now driving the top end of the modern furniture market. As chairs are increasingly being regarded as objects of desire rather than objects of utility, we are also coming to see ourselves as 'consumers of cultural products' rather than as users.

Look at me

It was the design historian Reyner Banham who coined the phrase 'furniturisation'. He was writing in the seminal catalogue for 'Modern Chairs 1918–70', an exhibition at the Whitechapel Art Gallery in the summer of 1970 . Banham evolved the term to describe a change that he recognised in the material world. A change in how previously unselfconscious and virtually invisible domestic artifacts – essentially the bibelot of everyday life, chairs, taps, cruets, etc – had suddenly become great design objects that demanded attention. Previously humble things were growing vast promotional superstructures that meshed beautifully with the rise of a culture of retail, celebrity and promotion.

Banham's text leans heavily on a Platonic ideal of technology, which imagines objects as human intention given perfect form. If I need to drive a nail into wood, the laminated leather handle, perfectly balanced forged Estwing 6oz claw hammer is indeed intention given form. It is a wonderful piece of technology perfected to drive and extract nails, and a beautiful thing as a consequence. Under this model of the material world, things cause the minimum of friction between my intention and its fulfilment. And in so doing, objects enable me to inhabit my environment – while making it in the image of my desire – as efficiently and pleasurably as possible. Like the vented stainless steel spout threaded through a cork – which can be inserted into any liquid condiment bottle to aid pouring – things that operate around perfect utility aspire to the status of invisibility. They operate below the level of everyday comprehension, while embodying the humility of a perfectly performed service.

Now I could not be – and neither was Banham – naive enough to think this self-effacing utility is, or should be the aspiration of every object, or a viable model for living in the world. And yet it's here, in the blind spot of a culture obsessed by promotion, that objects and the people associated with them accrue a kind of moral authority. There are few things more pleasurable than being able to luxuriate in the appropriateness of an object to a particular context.

Opposite
The Estwing claw hammer, high quality with invisible service.

35

To appreciate the way a handle fits the reaching hand and amplifies the torque necessary to open the door is a real joy. A joy that can send a shiver of recognition as the beauty of the object/gesture refracts through one's consciousness; like the Estwing hammer. The function of things is enhanced by our ability to become aware of an object, or to reflect, share and exchange those observations in moments of leisure, at a later time. This is what I'm doing now.

That objects exist in various mediums of exchange, while simultaneously fulfilling their function, is part of our commonsense, it's here that they evolve a communicative potential. Working with the Estwing hammer has a different status and coffers different status to the person using it, than, say, a hickory handled, cast not forged head claw-hammer; anyone familiar with using building tools would recognise the difference. And the fact that I previously described a pouring spout commonly used for olive oil, instantly marks me as comfortably middle class. Things, even in their perfect utility, become part of the means through which we interpret the world back to ourselves. Even something as simple as a change of context – imagine the Estwing as

evidence in a murder trial – opens up objects to varied interpretation and uses. Although it's in this gap, the lack of fit between an object's intention and its communicative possibility, where things become pray to 'furniturisation'. Shameless promotion has dissolved the moral authority of invisible service.

Later in his essay Banham suggests you become aware of what is under your arse when reading. I suggest you do the same now because the probability is that you are being supported by an object which offers many things, though self-effacing service is unlikely to be one of them. A painfully inappropriate chair, awkward, heavy, too hard, too thin, too expensive, red or whatever, invites the invisible 'design' of everyday practice, the playful appropriation, reuse and abuse of things. Chairs reserve parking spaces in the street, hold doors open, become clothes racks, table legs, temporary bookshelves, baby-changing platforms, or stepladders. In fact sitting seems one of the uses we least require of chairs, compared to the time they spend fulfilling other unintended functions. Fantastically comfortable chairs, invisible in their service, might not be so good at holding piles of magazines (they slide off the shiny angled seat onto the floor, ditto the ironing) or for hanging jackets and coats on (the weight pulls the chair over onto its back). The pleasure of the perfect things in action is complicated by the enormous value to be gained from the less-than-perfect object, which by a process of creative reuse finds its appropriate place in the world

Things are always already designed and reproduced on our behalf, by someone else, and we generally encounter them through our promotional culture of retail. A network of forces – design, reproduction and retail distribution – through which we are coerced into thinking of ourselves, not as articulate users or makers, but as consumers of cultural products. Adrift amongst the promotional themes in consumption, objects and people are merely relays for the rapid refreshment of capital; we buy, use and dispose of things with little regard for the quality of those exchanges. Objects that offer invisible service, or activate the creative reuse of things, operate in a blind spot in the evolution of retail culture. What people actually do with their latest purchase is a mystery, a mystery even to market analysis. Research can quantify what has been designed, produced and purchased, but post point-of-sale things disappear from the professional gaze of the media and enter their rich and varied lives. Back home, it is astonishing how often the product is a disappointment. Invariably it's too big, small, not powerful enough, doesn't work, they break, and frequently cost far too much money in the first place. I had to saw the ends from the legs of the new chairs so they fit under the table. And it is this failure that ushers in the vast reservoir of anonymous, transient

and perishable design – essentially the redesign and reuse of things through finding or adapting objects to carry out intentions they cannot fulfil, were never intended for, or never imagined existed. While this practice of everyday design is difficult to represent, it does not stop the expansionist culture of retail, constantly probing for a market to supply. Through a plethora of design, make-over and DIY television programmes, lifestyle and 'shelter' magazines, professional design – as the shock troops of retail culture – attempts to colonise, aestheticise and profit from the everyday. This inevitably accelerates the 'furniturisation' of every object, adding to the popular perception of there just being too much stuff, much too much stuff.

The 'furniturisation' identified by Banham has become the default setting for the vast avalanche of objects that pour from CAD programs, opportunity, a gap in the market, redirected capital flows, out through retail distribution only to finally haunt us as landfill. From salt shakers to cities, what these otherwise disparate objects share is their status as 'designed' intention. That is, objects whose principal function is to draw attention to themselves, and simultaneously distribute the

'brand' or signature of the designer who authorised their reproduction. It is a stunning inversion of all that we might have begun to identify as being beautiful about things: is it not perverse that a useless chromed object, a lemon juicer shaped like a 1930s idea of a spaceship becomes an icon of 'design' and an index of middle-class taste? The 'Starck' juicer, and other similar objects crystallise the trajectory towards self-reflexive objects; they intentionally exist outside of any recoverable use – too light even to masquerade as a doorstop – existing exclusively as advertising in a material form.

Surely, if we demand an ethical conduct in our patterns of consumption – through 'green' shopping, ethical investment and responsible end-use – there is an equal responsibility in the design and reproduction of things. We can no longer afford the luxury of manufacturing a world in which things perform as an endless spectacle. No longer can every teapot, chair, lemon squeezer and grommet merely shout 'look at me, look at me, look at me'. ⚙

Neil Cummings is an artist and Reader in Theory and Practice at Chelsea College of Art and Design. Two recent projects include a book, *The Value of Things* (August/Birkhauser), and the 'Free Trade' exhibition and related series of events at the recently reopened Manchester Art Gallery.

Opposite top and bottom
'No parking' and 'van-trailer'. Products are often being ingeniously adapted or reused. Chairs can become temporary parking cones or old vans can be transformed into trailers.

Above top left and right
Philippe Starck's collander and lemon juicer presented in their branded environment.

Above bottom left
'Alessi and Authentics' in a London department store.

Alvaro Siza

Tradition, Modernism and the Banal

In an interview with **Edwin Heathcote**, the Portuguese Modernist architect Alvaro Siza expresses his desire to produce furniture that is inspired by 'banality' and the everyday. Heathcote reflects how this culminates in his subtle and distinct designs, and questions him on why he chooses traditional materials and craftsmanship over more innovative techniques.

In a 1933 lecture, Auguste Perret said:

> the architect who…creates a work that will always seem to have existed, that is, in a word, 'banal', is entitled to feel content. This is because the goal of Art is not to astonish or to move us; astonishment and excitement are like brief shocks – contingent, trivial emotions. The true goal of Art is to lead us dialectically from one pleasure to the next, beyond admiration into pure delight.[1]

This word 'banal' is one which seems to crop up with frequency in the architectural discourse of Modernism. It is also a word which Alvaro Siza has used to describe his work. It is an odd word because, from the outside, it seems to indicate a notion of the boring, the everyday, the dull. To many architects, however, it has represented a kind of release. Adolf Loos once wrote: 'When we come across a mound in the woods, six feet long and three feet wide raised to a pyramidal form by a spade we become serious and something in us says: someone was buried here. That is architecture'.[2] To Loos, that pile of earth could express more than the most elaborate building. Siza, when writing about Loos's design for a bentwood chair said: 'Adolf Loos's reflections on design are important and contemporary: they emphasise the fact that necessity, not art, is the spur for the design of a perfect object. The Thonet chair designed by Loos is wonderful. Looking at it, you can tell without further ado:

"That is a Thonet chair"'.[3]

Loos's chair was designed for the Café Museum in Vienna in 1899. So lacking was this interior in decoration (completed as it was at the height of the decorative frenzy of the Wiener Secession) that it was soon nicknamed the Café Nihilismus. Loos was delighted by the slight. A nihilist chair for a nihilist coffee house in a city that Loos's friend, Karl Kraus, had described as 'the laboratory for the end of the world'.

Loos's chair was a stripped-down version of what was already a stripped-down chair, the No. 14 Chair, designed by Michael Thonet in 1859 (50 million of which had been sold by 1930). Yet it is by no means minimal – compared to Loos's pared-down buildings its curves seem almost luxurious. It has just enough sexy residual curves not to draw attention to itself as a self-consciously minimal object and is just comfortable enough not to be truly nihilistic. It is interesting to note that Loos, despite his skeletal design for Thonet, did not like self-consciously modern chairs. In his buildings he invariably used traditional designs, either English archetypes like Chipperfield, Hepplewhite or plump Chesterfields, or occasionally a stuffy Biedermeier-type armchair or basic Thonet chairs. In this predilection for the ordinary and the conservative he shied away from anything that proclaimed its Modernist credentials.

Siza's furniture, like Loos's Thonet chair, is stripped down, extremely (although deceptively) simple, a little fragile, but never what you would call Modernist or Minimalist. I asked him how he approaches the design of a chair:

Opposite
Alvaro Siza, Church of Santa Maria in Marco de Canavezes (1990–96). Siza designed the simple chairs for his church.

Above left
Alvaro Siza, self-portrait in mirror.

Above right
Sketches for Borges and Irmao Bank and Chairs for Bank, 1978. Studies for Chairs, 1985.

The most important thing about the chair is
that it should look like a chair – have the
character and personality of a chair. The first
chairs I designed were meant for specific
spaces, for houses I was designing at the time
and they were heavily related to the buildings,
to the architecture. A piece of furniture must
stand well in a particular house but it must
also have a strength and a quality which will
allow it to go anywhere. It also needs a type of
modesty which will allow it to be used and to
last, a banality.

If it is the everyday, the 'banal' which Siza is
after, what kind of furniture, was he inspired by?

I have the idea that a chair is a very old
object. If you look at Ancient Egyptian chairs,
they're very similar to modern designs, so I
look toward traditional chairs. I like old
American chairs, made by the Shakers and
also the chairs you see in villages in Portugal
and Spain. In fact the craftsmen who make
my chairs in Portugal spend most of their
time making traditional and classical chairs,
they are excellent, highly skilled and it shows
that there is little difference in technique in

making a modern chair or in making one of my
designs.

Siza tends to use traditional materials:

Despite the arrival of new materials, the human body
is more or less the same as it has always been. By
making a chair in wood, you can make a chair that
looks like a chair. There are so many designs that
just try to be original and that don't look anything
like chairs. These lose something, the essence. By
changing small details, or proportion you can do a lot
with the design. ...My designs start off sometimes
quite elaborate. Then the design becomes simpler, it
develops and in the end, what is left is the essence.

In an essay, Siza has written of the design of the
chair: 'In order to express a certain uniqueness, without
betraying its essence, it is important to ensure that the
design does not run the risk of being too obvious. In this
way it can assume a touch of originality that might be
discreetly attractive, while remaining "banal" at the
same time. Starting out obsessed with originality shows
an uncouth and superficial attitude.'[4]

Of all Siza's furniture designs, perhaps the one which
is most refined and most fully combines his notion of an
archetypal 'essence' and a stripped-down 'banality' is
the chair designed for the Church at Marco de

Canavezes (1990–96). In this building he combines elements of the local Baroque -influenced church vernacular with his characteristic spartan Mediterranean architectonic language. Siza designed all the furniture for the church and it is the furniture which humanises the space, which brings human scale to an otherwise austere, extremely cool interior.

Initially the chair looks like the epitome of Siza's notion of the essential chair, but on closer inspection its structure is relatively complex, the stretchers and bracing of the legs creating a convoluted set of spaces beneath the seat. The line of the stretcher between the front and rear legs is continued out to become a kneeler at the rear; the effect is rather akin to that of stabilisers on a bike – as well as rooting the piece of furniture to the ground it makes it into a piece of furniture to be engaged with by two people. From the slight S-curve of the back to the tapering section of the backrest, from the staggered series of stretchers to the H-shaped lateral brace, there is a subtle complexity which marks the chair out as a work of great modesty and thoughtfulness, yet which retains its banality in relation to this initial appearance which, quite frankly, evokes nothing more glamorous than a kitchen chair.

The same ordinariness can be found in his folding chairs of 1973, the C1 chair of 1985 (a little more self-consciously minimal), and Mare table and chair of 1997, as well as in his pared -down designs for ironmongery and the dressing-table drawer and mirror, Espelho 2. The 1992 design for a chest of drawers (Comoda 2) is a little more complex; an entirely flush front accommodates a slide-out surface and three drawers. The piece relies on the craftsmanship of its construction to maintain its simplicity and elegance.

Siza says of this craftsmanship:
...the craftsmen we have here are very good but they work with traditional techniques and technology. In this way, there is nothing to stimulate me to use new materials. I recently designed a table which is being manufactured in Italy. Originally I designed it for an exhibition of my work, and models and drawings were displayed on the table's surface. An Italian company decided to put the table into production. It looks like a simple, obvious table but it's actually very hard to construct because of the length. If you look at it, it looks unlikely that it would stand up but because of a sophisticated steel structure

Footnotes
1. Karla Britton, *Auguste Perret*, Phaidon (London), 2002, p 243.
2. *The Architecture of Adolf Loos*, Arts Council, Exhibition Catalogue, London 1985, p 88.
3. Kenneth Frampton, *Alvaro Siza: Complete Works*, Phaidon Press (London), 2000, p 597.
4. Ibid.

I'm not particularly afraid of this phantasm of losing identity. If we are so weak as to be dominated, then we deserve to lose our tradition. Portugal has a history of change and foreign influence, some of our best buildings were built by Italians and there has always been the influence of the East.

underneath it manages to support itself. The Italians use technology and materials very well – if I was designing there I am sure I would be designing very different things and using different materials.

But he isn't. Siza is identified with a very particular strain of what Kenneth Frampton has identified as 'critical regionalism' and, along with Fernando Tavora and Eduardo Souto de Moura, he has set an example of modesty and consistency in modern and design architecture since the 1950s. Yet, he does not see his work as particularly Portuguese and is not worried by a weakening of the Mediterranean tradition of Modernist design: 'I'm not particularly afraid of this phantasm of losing identity. If we are so weak as to be dominated, then we deserve to lose our tradition. Portugal has a history of change and foreign influence, some of our best buildings were built by Italians and there has always been the influence of the East.'

Siza calls himself a traditionalist, a conservative. He thinks of himself as part of a Mediterranean, a Portuguese and an international tradition which reduces vernacular or banal elements to their essence. He shares with Loos a love of the unpretentious, the vernacular and the pared-down, and with Max Bill the delight in the beauty of the ordinary and the everyday. His furniture, like his architecture, is subtle and self-effacing, but he remains aware of its quality. When I ask whether he sees himself as part of a Portuguese tradition in design he answers: 'Well, I'd hope my work generates a new tradition.' We all would. ᗄ

Top
Bed and day bed designed by
John Pawson for Italian
furniture manufacturer Driade.

Bottom and both opposite top
Images of John Pawson's
bench and day bed in the
Pawson House.

Opposite bottom
Portrait of John Pawson.

42

Preferential
Treatments

John Pawson Recommends the Work of AG Fronzoni and Maarten van Severen

The master of reductivism **John Pawson** describes how his starting point for furniture is always the first principles of a piece's essence rather than other people's prototypes. Regarding furniture design as a facet of the total vision that architecture offers, he recommends the work of two architects – the Italian AG Fronzoni (1923–2002) and Belgian designer Maarten van Severen.

My approach with any commission is always to start from scratch, taking nothing as a given – there is every reason to reinvent the wheel, so long as you come up with a better wheel. If I am designing a chair, I do not think about what other people have produced and set about modifying these archetypes. Instead I start from first principles – what is the essence of a chair and what is the optimal three-dimensional form for this essence? I refine and reduce my ideas, paring away until what is left cannot be improved by further subtraction. I enjoy the discipline of pushing simplicity and clarity to their limits, seeking the comfort of exactness, of absolute precision of scale and detailing – there is a vast difference between something which has the quality of simplicity and something which is crude.

I like to work with as few materials as possible – restrict the palette and you reduce the number and distraction of junctions. The goal is absolute visual comfort – a condition of seamlessness, where nothing stops the eye. My preference is for natural materials – stone, wood, metal, glass. I like the sense that the material continues beyond the surface, beyond what can actually be seen.

For the Cistercian monastery I have designed in Bohemia, I am working on simple wooden pieces which will sit comfortably within a context of white plaster walls and polished concrete floors.

As an architect, I regard furniture design as the reverse of diversification. I am interested in architecture which offers a total vision. Everything must be considered, as anything which is placed within a space has an impact – not just furniture, even something as apparently insignificant as a light switch.

On Maarten van Severen

The quality of directness van Severen achieves appeals to me – the sense that he is dealing with the essence of things. You look at his work and think why did no-one think of that before, but the simplicity is deceptive – the processes which have culminated in any one of his rigorously refined pieces are anything but simple. This is true of both the concept and its physical realisation – the finished form may look basic, but, in terms of the detailing, is almost always extremely complex.

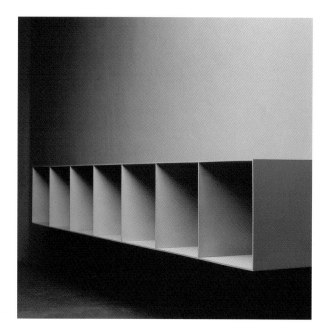

Top
Solid aluminium bookcase
(1990).

Bottom left
Wooden table (1988).

Bottom right
Birch plywood oiled chairs
(1993).

On AG Fronzoni

I treasure the Fronzoni pieces I have, not least because they are tangible reminders of an extraordinary man. His work perfectly illustrates how things can be at once uncompromisingly rigorous and lyrical. His designs are exercises in absolute reduction, free of all superfluous gesture. Functional issues are pared down to their essential, almost anonymous minimum. The work is characterised by an intellectual quality – his furniture has more to do with satisfying the mind than with providing physical comfort. Interestingly, unlike the work of many designers, Fronzoni's pieces fit beautifully within many different kinds of architecture – never invisible, but never jarring either. △D

Top
AG Fronzoni, desk for La Polena Gallery, Genoa.

Bottom
AG Fronzoni, table in Van Royen Apartment.

Four Projects by David Adjaye
The Concept of Furniture

Over the last year, David Adjaye has become one of the most celebrated young architects in London. High-profile clients, such as Ewan McGregor and artists Jake Chapman and Chris Ofili, have meant that his work has become a focus of attention for broadsheet colour supplements and interior magazines, as well as the architectural press. Unswayed by success, Adjaye remains consistent in his direction and his approach. Along with the influx of glamorous interiors commissions, his office is designing two community projects for libraries in Tower Hamlets, one of London's poorest inner-city boroughs. An important attribute of his architecture is its relationship to his bespoke furniture designs – both freestanding and built in **Peter Allison** looks at four of his recent projects in detail and explains how in Adjaye's spaces 'the concept of furniture' goes beyond the actual design of setpieces, with his treatment of specific architectural elements being more akin to furniture design than conventionally architectural design.

In David Adjaye's architecture, furniture and the concept of furniture play a decisive role in three main ways: in the design of tables and chairs which occupy key positions in many of his projects; in the design of larger-scale storage units, which may be freestanding or integrated with the surrounding fabric; and in an approach to the design of certain architectural elements in which they are treated like items of furniture. The tables and chairs are normally made of timber and form simple rectangular compositions the outline of which recalls earlier models but lacks historic detail. Many of the tables are cantilevered at both ends, giving the long axis more importance than the shorter cross-axis, whilst the chairs, with their asymmetrical side elevations, face in one direction only. With a dark stained finish, they are both visually distinctive and sympathetic to close contact.

In the context of Adjaye's architecture, their purpose is to provide the minimum level of support for each project to be brought into use; beyond this point his clients are expected to select their own furniture, based on their response to the environment they have commissioned. A project overlooking Kensington Palace Gardens in London, the KPG apartment, provides a clear demonstration of this strategy where Adjaye has designed the main dining table and chairs, as well as the beds, and the client has provided other furniture in response to the scale and finishes of different spaces. It is also worth noting that Adjaye's involvement here extended to the design of a profiled bath and basins in Ficore. His readiness to use a variety of materials in the furniture and fittings of his

projects, together with a permissive attitude to the relationship between different pieces, has some similarities with the work of Eileen Gray.

The role of storage in Adjaye's architecture is partly a product of his appreciation of Japanese culture which began with an eight-month study visit when he was a student. As the floor of a tatami room can be used for different functions by day and night, the provision of storage, normally situated behind sliding panels, enables the space to be quickly transformed from one state to another. In several domestic projects, he has reworked this model and, in commissions involving combinations of storage and display, he has investigated its potential in other situations. In the KPG apartment, storage and service volumes play a decisive role in the definition of space and its animation in detail. Two walls of each of the main bedrooms are formed by storage which, internally, meets the needs of the client and, externally, continues the timber lining of the other walls. Lower in height, a stainless steel bench occupies a structural bay, just inside the east facade, and includes the more active components of the kitchen. Food storage and a utility room are incorporated in the parallel volume, which also includes lifts and staircases, behind a continuous bank of doors. A similar use of storage and service elements to define architectural space can be seen in the work of Mies van der Rohe, especially in residential projects such as the Farnsworth House.

Both the freestanding furniture and the storage volumes are designed so that their proportions and organisation are easy to read and understand. Their limits are well defined and there is a clear relationship between each component and the larger organisation of which it is part. If this type of understanding informs his

47

approach to furniture, it also plays a significant role in Adjaye's architecture. Although demonstrating an overall unity of purpose, the architecture is often composed of large-scale elements whose geometry and materiality demonstrate a high degree of independence. These elements tend to come in pairs and their differences complement one another, producing a charged field in the intervening space. There are several examples in the KPG apartment. The fixed Privalite glazing on the west facade, which can be switched from transparent to translucent depending on whether there is a current passing through the gas in the void of the glazing units, is paired with the folding and sliding glazing on the east facade. Similarly, the roof plane is perforated by a pattern of generous rooflights which, with natural light by day and artificial by night, illuminate key areas of the floor plane below. Both the ceiling and floor are designed with recessed and upstanding margins respectively, as if to signal their differences and their compatibility.

In most of Adjaye's projects, the balance between the three main elements, freestanding furniture, storage and service volumes, and architectural elements conceived like furniture, is not equal and one or two of them play a more dominant role, depending on context and programme. The inherent flexibility of this approach can be demonstrated by a comparison of three projects with quite different functions: Social, a bar located in an older building in central London; the Elektra House in London's East End; and a shop interior for Browns Focus collection in London's West End.

At Social, the largest space, in the basement, is activated by the relative positions of two service and display volumes, a double-height bar at the street end and a low stage at the other. Both side walls are clad in vertical panels of backlit GRP which are reminiscent of strip windows, except that one continues inside the space whilst the other passes into an external light-well containing an escape stair. Like a geometric landscape, slight differences in level create a series of secondary spaces which retain a degree of independence.

At a lower level, one side of a small dance floor is occupied by light steel furniture which, at other times, is easily stacked away. Along a low terrace next to the dance floor, the parapet and a series of tables and benches have been cast in insitu concrete, continuing the landscape idea. On the side wall, a cast concrete bench, with narrow tables, looks back across the space; in both cases there are leather cushions on the seats. A lighter leather is used to upholster the U-shaped seating which forms five booths in the ground-floor bar, which is oak-lined and has no windows, where various devices have been used to admit external light to the basement. Each booth has a substantial steel table and independently controlled lighting. Hinting at the changefulness and variety of the interior, the street facade consists of a steel and glass screen which can slide open when required.

In the second example, the Elektra House, the living room includes a dining table and a steel stool and daybed designed by Adjaye, and other pieces collected by the owners but, on a constricted site, the position of service and storage volumes play a crucial role in its practical and spatial organisation. At ground level, the kitchen has been placed in a small appendage on one side of the main house so that the main living space occupies a single, unbroken volume with dramatic shifts in scale and lighting at different points on the section. On the first floor, the provision of three bedrooms has only been possible on the basis that each of them has its own floor-to-ceiling storage and is just big enough to accommodate a bed. In other respects, the powerful presence of this small house lies in the polarisation of the various planes which account for its design.

On a street of modest Victorian houses, a windowless facade in dark brown phenolic ply, with an internal face of white-painted plaster, is paired with a facade which is physically and visually open but offers no view except for a small courtyard and the sky above. Horizontally, the house is cut by three planes with similar areas but entirely different programmes. The ground floor has an epoxy finish to the concrete screed and, on the open side, rises up to form a window seat, on the level of the external court, and fixed seating on two sides of the dining table. The first floor, suspended within the volume delineated by the ground floor, provides very limited views and supports three bed spaces and has a bathroom in one corner. Light and air for these spaces are provided by the plane above, the roof, which incorporates six rooflights the size and orientation of which match the spaces below. The interaction between these elements produces a wide range of conditions within a comparatively small volume and provides a model for a more self-contained and ecologically friendly future.

The subtle zoning of space in both Social and the Elektra House is achieved largely on the basis of

screening off significant aspects of the surrounding area. This has been taken to new levels in the interior for Browns Focus collection in London's West End. Situated at street and basement levels, a single interior has been created in the space between two storage and display systems, each capable of forming distinctive volumes at a smaller scale. A folded screen in panels of normal, tinted and sandblasted mirror follows the outer wall on the upper level, enclosing a control panel and changing room as it does so. An internal ring of storage and display is formed by the deep parapet surrounding a central stair. Carefully detailed in Paralam, a structural material made from waste timber products, its angled face and inclined top reflect the geometry of the outer screen and provide visual support for the Paralam staircase which descends to the lower floor, without actually touching it. From a position just inside the main entrance, a glass-walled display cabinet in the front face of this parapet shows the stair descending to a point immediately below.

At basement level, the staircase is embedded in a host volume with faceted changing rooms and angled shelves to either side. On the opposite wall, four low, arched tunnels extend beneath the pavement above; two of them are used for display, with a field of dishes set at ascending heights, and two provide further hanging space and are fully accessible. Their walls and those of the dressing rooms are also clad in three types of mirror. In front of the non-accessible tunnels, a faceted, leather-clad bench embraces the foot of the staircase in a relationship that unifies the otherwise polarised spaces at each level. Representing the base colours in fashion design, the ground floor is predominantly black, with a black terrazzo floor

and a black Parasol ceiling, and the lower level is predominantly white. Whilst the ground floor expands the periphery around a central point which cannot be occupied without descending to the floor below, the longer views in the basement can be appreciated from the calm of a central space. This is an interior in which collective spectacle and individual gaze are both possible.

The recombination of similar elements in widely different compositions has all the characteristics of a continuing research programme. In the majority of Adjaye's projects, a limited number of materials, used in unbroken planes, determine the predominant colour and atmosphere. Most elements are conceived in wall and floor-sized units in which the visual, rather than the physical, texture of the surface predominates, a distinction which is perhaps most clear in the work of Adolf Loos. Junctions, where they occur, are detailed as simple abutments. In a cluttered world, these gently assembled planes clear a space which has the potential to address the most substantial aspects of the brief. In this respect, the scale of the furniture provides a direct counterpoint to the spatial composition of Adjaye's projects. The spaces themselves have an ambiguity of scale and orientation; the ceiling in the living area of the KPG apartment has the appearance of a stone pavement, for instance. In contrast, the dimensions of the furniture relate directly to the human body and their abstract detailing refers to the design of the environment in which they are located. In the case of the storage units and the architectural elements conceived as furniture, the connection with the body becomes more remote as the scale approaches that of the building. This sequence of spatial linkages may be extended outwards, to the surrounding area, and inwards to the scale of a utensil or implement.

In Adjaye's architecture, the attention to detail is intended to direct attention away from physical questions towards an awareness of organisational possibilities and their relevance to a larger programme. In this context, the position and distribution of the furniture and furniture-based elements continue this process by suggesting a number of more detailed scenarios. ⌀

Peter Allison trained at the Architectural Association. He contributes to several publications and has curated recent exhibitions on Austrian architecture and new work from London. He teaches in London.

Project 1 KPG apartment

Adjaye Associates, KPG
apartment, London 2002
In this scheme, Adjaye
renovated a 1960s penthouse
flat in Kensington Palace
Garden for a businessman.
An important aspect of the
project was finding a way to
encompass the client's
substantial art collection,
which includes Biedermeier
furniture and Oriental objects.
By dividing the flat into two
distinct parts – public and
private – a means was found
to display the objects in the
public rooms – living room,
dining room, kitchen, library
and terrace.

Top right
Main bathroom with
freestanding profiled bath
in Ficore.

Middle right
Guest bedroom with floor,
lining and bed in sycamore,
and folding, sliding glazing
to park.

Bottom left
Entrance skylight with
matching floor and ceiling
planes in Portuguese
limestone, and fixed
Privalite glazing.

Project 2 Social Club

Adjaye and Russell, Social, London 1999
David Adjaye designed this bar in central London with former partner William Russell. Largely situated below ground, the main space is bound by a stage at one end and a bar at the street end. Despite the parameters, furniture is used to create a variety of spaces that can be changed according to shifting patterns of use.

Above
The basement level. Both side walls are clad in vertical panels of backlit GRP. The parapet and a series of tables and benches have been cast in insitu concrete.

Below left
Lighter leather upholsters the U-shaped seating booths in the oak-lined ground-floor bar.

Below right top
Basement plan.

Below right bottom
Ground-floor plan.

Project 3 Elektra House

Adjaye Associates, Elektra House, East London 2001
This house within the existing walls of an existing building, a one-storey belt factory, was designed for an artist and a sculptor and their two children. For structural economy, existing boundaries, walls and foundations were made use of. A new steel frame was inserted from which was hung the facades and a roof space for accommodating the bedrooms. The new, light, south facade was constructed out of resin-coated plywood, while the insulated north facade has no aspect.

Above left and bottom right
The north and south facades are designed as complementary elements, with no windows to the street and a large area of glazing to the south.

Above right
The south facade also defines the dining area and a small court.

Bottom left
Plan.

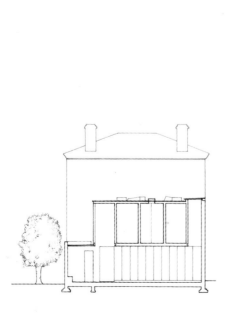

Project 4 Browns Focus

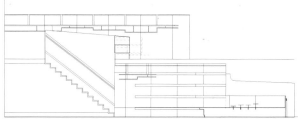

Adjaye Associates, Browns Focus, London 2002
At Browns Focus, two distinct environments were created that were designed around the needs of the shopper. The first being a kaleidoscopic room of mirror lights conceived for multiplicity, reflection and gazing, and the second a white space of exhibition for decision making and ultimately purchase.

Above left
View from entrance with glazed display cabinet revealing handrail to staircase. The solid Paralam parapet complements the peripheral wall in three types of mirrored glass.

Middle right
Section.

Right
Lower floor showing mirror-clad changing rooms.

The Cultural
Divide

The late 20th century was characterised by a cultural divide between furniture design and architecture. **Alison Brooks** speculates what benefits might come with the blurring and convergence of the two previously distinct disciplines. She anticipates what the future now holds specifically through a discussion of her own work at Alison Brooks Associates (ABA) and through her recommendation of Jam, an office that first established its reputation through its engagement with issues of recycling and has since shifted towards working with manufacturers' brands and explicitly using 'design to communicate'.

Opposite
ABA, 'Shelf Life' designed and prototyped for the Atoll Hotel, Germany.

Top
Mario Botta's 1982 Prima chair by Alias. Coinciding with the 1980s birth of designer consumerism, the geometric purity and structural elegance of the Prima was a sea change from Botta's Memphis/Sottsass work.

Above
Alison Brooks portrait.

Having spent seven years (1989–96) in close working proximity to one of the great furniture designers of the late 20th century, I had the advantage of viewing the world of furniture design from the architect's 'side' and the world of architecture from the designer's 'side'. From what I could tell, these two sides were, in the late 1980s and early 1990s, mutually suspicious of and even opposed to the other's products, cultural perspective and working methods. During the past 10 years there has been a gradual opening and convergence of the two disciplines; there is no longer an exclusionist perspective on furniture, architecture and art. I believe there is still room for more interdependence and cross-fertilisation, and this is a subject that has been at the heart of ABA's ventures into furniture design.

While working with Arad I was exposed to the designer's attitude that architects were out of touch with materials, distanced from the process of making, ignorant of contemporary (and historical) movements in art and oblivious to the potential dialogue between these fields of activity (all true). Architects (even the 'good' Modernists as opposed to the 'bad' Post-Modernists) were too steeped in convention to appreciate the poetry, whimsy and

conceptual/material experiments that furniture designers were producing. On the other hand was the architect's stock criticism of designers' apparent disdain for the 'modern project', to bring good modern design at an affordable price to the masses, to carry out really useful societal problem-solving through design. This paradigm has been neglected since the Arts and Crafts movement, the Bauhaus and perhaps the Danish/Eames experiments with plywood production. Reinforcing this disdain were lines of division in the media – the furniture design pages were always found at the back of architectural publications, like the riff -raff sitting in the back row of the class, easy to ignore.

I remember talking with Ron Arad about one of the first pieces of furniture that made it out of the 1980s and into the architectural limelight – Mario Botta's 1982 Prima chair by Alias. It had a geometric purity and structural elegance that was a sea change from the Memphis/Sottsass work, while around the same time Gehry made his Experimental Armchair in Cardboard and 'architecture' suddenly took note. These chairs accompanied the birth of 'designer' consumerism in the 1980s with Starck and the Alessi phenomenon bringing the iconic 'designed' household object back into the public realm. However these were not destined to improve the lifestyle of the less-than-affluent – the new 'project' brought design only to the disposable-incoming middle classes.

It seems that despite these exclusive beginnings the 'trickle-down effect' of the 1980s and 1990s designer revolution has worked. No self-respecting restaurant or domestic interior is complete without its stock of Vitra/Jacobsen chairs, and Ikea now brings affordable 'modern design' to the masses. At the 1999 Milan Furniture Fair Ikea took the show by storm, introducing its PS line in a fashionably semi-derelict warehouse – shockingly, many of the pieces indistinguishable from those by the Italian minimalist supremos. The elitism/ inaccessibility of designer furniture was exposed and the top echelon of manufacturers were suddenly afraid of the dent Ikea might make in their market. But it turns out that no real 'socialising' impact was made on the design industry by Ikea's invasion of Milan, except for the emergence of Starck's super-cheap plastic chairs by Vitra. Yet they still don't seem to turn up in council-flat kitchens or the local caff.

The design-industry manufacturers continue to bank their profits on the value the designer 'signature' adds to their product and increasingly, rather than a means of self-expression or real use, consumers buy designer furniture as investments.

In the main, design-industry manufacturers continue to bank their profits on the value the designer 'signature' adds to their product and increasingly, rather than a means of self-expression or real use, consumers buy designer furniture as investments. There are a few young designers who address issues of recycling and basic shelter, like Jam; some who poetically manipulate simple materials, like Baldele and Heatherwick; others who are beginning to make environmentally friendly objects.

In 1974 Ingo Maurer heard about a chemical spill in Japan that destroyed the livelihood of a community of seaweed-harvesters – formerly *uchiwa* (fan) makers. He approached the villagers with a series of designs for lamps using the *uchiwa*. The manufacture of these lamps, a huge 1970s success, revived a disappearing art and employed 21 villagers for many years. Our 'global village' clearly holds limitless opportunities like this to invent new objects that not only add poetry and joy to our lives but also address humanitarian issues and renew skills. (This does not imply manufacturers taking new furniture 'shapes' to the Far East to be made cheaply in rattan and wicker sweatshops.) A little more social idealism and diversity can't hurt.

Left top
Ron Arad's early 1990s line of sprung/tempered steel furniture is a joyful species that exploits the mechanics of sprung steel and counterbalancing.

Left middle
Ingo Maurer, Uchiwa (fan) Lamp, 1974. A huge design success, this lamp also illustrates the humanitarian potential of carefully positioned projects. The lamps were produced for Maurer by a Japanese community of former *uchiwa* (fan) makers, whose livelihood was threatened by a chemical spill.

Opposite top and middle
Drawing and images of 'Shelf-Life' being manufactured the all in one unit for the Atoll Hotel, Germany.

Opposite bottom
ABA's first project to convert a compact 19th-century pub shown in section.

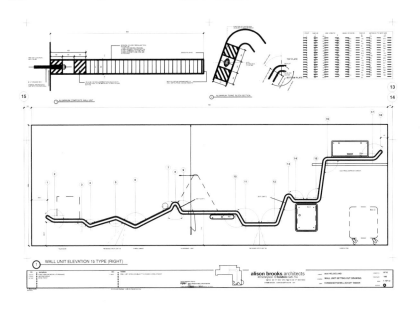

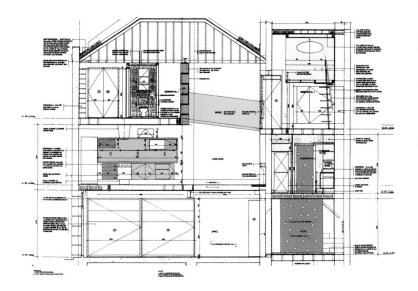

Cross Fertilisation, Hybrid Objects and Space-Saving

Maybe as a result of this long period of observation and speculation about the nature of the designer and the furniture industry, ABA's work in furniture has always shied away from the consumer-object-spectacle. Our work either tries to disguise itself as part of the architectural backdrop, the spatial canvas, or as multi-functional pieces that blur the distinction between architecture and furniture. We are interested in carrying on the tradition of built-in furniture that extends architecture into the tactile realm of the body. The architectural scale is reduced but the ideas reinforced, space more precisely tailored to movement, touch, sight and human contact. Thus our preoccupation with the bench rather than the chair, the moving object rather than the static, the multi-purpose rather than the single-function.

Childhood experience probably plays a role in these preoccupations - the first piece of furniture that inspired my fascination was a 1923, white-painted pressed-steel rocking sofa which lived in the screened porch of my Canadian summer cottage. This slightly rusting, squeaking object is complete with ski-like legs, cast iron levers for adjusting the degree of swing, naugahyde cushions and two sprung steel cantilevered armchairs to match. Intriguingly adjustable, this animate, machinic object works with body weight and motion to create a memorable 'ride'. Ron Arad's early 1990s line of sprung/tempered steel furniture (No Spring Chicken, Reitveld, Beware of the Dog etc.) are of a similar joyful species that exploits the mechanics of sprung steel and counterbalancing.

One of ABA's first projects was the conversion of a compact 19th-century Brighton pub building to a home for a structural engineer. By eliminating the upper middle floor of the three-storey building a double-height space was created with one bedroom a mezzanine open to the living spaces below. The balustrade for this bedroom became a fibreglass 'library' that could be lowered via pulleys to become a wall separating living and kitchen areas below. The kitchen island could be rotated to face the living area, both areas lined with a continous storage bench for infinite dining table locations. The sloping roof/ceiling of the child's bedroom was 'peeled' off to become an elevated bed, a suspended timber platform accessed through a hole. When space is 3-dimensionally 'freed', furniture can perform a double or triple function, modulating space to use and vice versa.

Jam

The name Jam is derived from the Christian names of its three founding partners, Jamie, Astrid and Matthieu, and a shared belief that collective thought is more powerful than the individual. With training in architecture, fine art and design, the trio moved to London and created a partnership in 1995. Jam's earliest work was radical and experimental in its nature. It pushed the boundaries of design through its exploration of materials and unique aesthetics. It quickly brought Jam into the limelight of contemporary culture, developing international awareness for what the trio were achieving through their challenging work.

Jam continued to develop its offering. Whereas before it had been about design and innovation, in 1997 it shifted to one of 'design to communicate'. This incorporated all the aspects of the previous work, however, Jam was now invited by manufacturing brands to look at how organisations could use their existing resources in new and different ways. The subsequent design and communication activities began having a profound impact on both organisational culture and the marketplace. Successful projects included working with Whirlpool, Sony and SGB Youngman. Each project promoted the brand in a unique and memorable way. Through association with Jam, the collaborative brand was able to obtain a cultural currency it would not have been able to attain through conventional marketing.

One of the earliest collaborations saw Jam develop a collection of furniture made from the stainless steel drum of Whirlpool's washing machines. These were used in interiors and sold through galleries as

Top
The Jam team at the launch of the Audi/Jam collaborative range on 22 February 2002 at the AUDI Forum. Jam are sitting on an Audi/Jam TT Bench, made from carbon fibre and TT roll bars. From left to right: Lee Kew-Moss, Astrid Zala, Jamie Anley, Damon De Ionno and Justin Leahy. Astrid and Jamie are the founders of the company.

Right (both images)
SGB Youngman, 1996–1998. Jam worked with SGB, Britain's leading ladder producer, to create a range of furniture that displayed the light, yet strong qualities of its ladder products.

functional objects in their own right. The Youngman collaboration gave birth to a collection of lightweight aluminium designs, celebrating their ladder technology. This was launched as the 'nineties' version of the Macintosh Ladder back chair. An understanding and skill set in the practice of design and architecture has given Jam a unique quality when forging its offer as a future communications- and brand-building team.

The Jam approach today brings alive a brand or organisation in a transformational way. This approach is called brand evolution and is achieved by capturing the essence of an organisation, through a deep understanding of its values, purpose and vision. It has grown from Jam's previous experience, but is no longer limited to manufacturing-based brands or organisations, rather all those that have a brand

that needs evolving in new and more experiential ways.

The brand evolution projects conceived and delivered, result from a unique process that has been developed over the last seven years. The initiatives provide a catalyst for a whole range of internal and external communication activities, from word-of-mouth to PR and advertising.

Many people give names to the form of brand evolution that Jam offers today – experiential, brand extension, emotional, etc. Although combining these elements, Jam's approach is genuinely different, having grown out of pioneering work using design as a communications tool, coupled to the simple understanding that audiences are increasingly influenced by brand activity that has integrity and value beyond the unusual and innovative.

Jam now works with a number of global brand leaders and smaller future-focused companies, on a myriad of brand evolution projects.

Above right and bottom right
The AUDI (Audi Uncovered Design Initiative), 2002.
Within the automotive sector Audi is synonymous with design. The initial collaboration between Audi and Jam in 2001 was focused on exploring, expressing and energising the brand. This was to be undertaken so that both staff and customers alike could interact and be motivated by the design theme central to the Audi brand. By conducting a research and ideation period, Jam was able to conceive more than just an experiential campaign to run in showrooms. The Audi brand evolution project, centred on design pieces inspired not only by components, but Audi technology, has helped provide Audi with a legitimate story behind the design ethos of the brand. It has helped provide a catalyst for marketing activities including advertising and public relations, where the brand can live the design value on many levels. The images here are a few of the resulting prototype pieces.

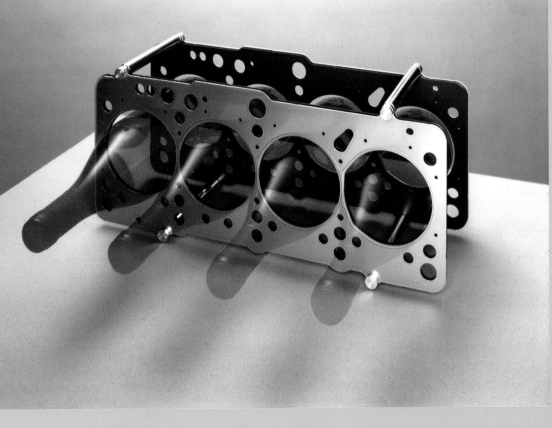

Realm of the senses

The commission for the Atoll Hotel in Germany was the opportunity to reconsider hotel furniture in the context of a 'total environment', where ABA could create a smooth space informed by the metaphor of a floating, man-made atoll. The first subject of our operation was the hotel room – hotel rooms are always disappointing, the most exciting bit usually being finding the minibar. They should satisfy childlike desires for adventure and surprise, exotic yet efficient. Thus we replaced the usual identity parade of pseudo-domestic furniture with one continuous 7-metre long structure cantilevered from the wall. This floor-free element, 'Shelf Life', is at once the closet/hanging rail, mini bar, suitcase rack/bench, desk, chaise longue and TV table. The erratic line of the unit on the wall gives it its stiffness by creating a series of lever arms, allowing it to be hung from nine bolts anchored into the wall at the 'peaks' of the bends.

Although manufactured from carbon fibre – both structural and finish material – these units with their accompanying internal wiring, lighting and suspended storage 'boxes' cost about £3600 each – far less than the cost of buying all the pieces of furniture separately. The unit was designed in three pieces for ease of handling, all fixings are concealed within the 60-millimetre thickness of the carbon-fibre skins/polyester foam core, and with a load of 15 men sitting along its length 'Shelf Life' only deflects by 2 millimetres at each end. Each unit was fabricated from three timber plugs and six plywood moulds – three moulds for the bottom skins and three for the top skins. The high-tech image disguises the s-low-tech process of fabricating the moulds and hand-laying/laminating each fragile sheet of carbon fibre. In the workshop each mould looked like a patient in an operating theatre undergoing delicate plastic surgery.

Beds are the *raison d'être* of hotels, the crux of the experience. How can a bed be responsive, animated, sexy and clean at the same time? Our ambition was at all costs to avoid the soft, too-vertical headboards that have cushioned strange and undesirable heads and backs, and to eliminate the altar-like symmetry of bedside table lamps. 'Let There Be Light' was born from these questions – a bed with wall-mounted self-illuminating headboard, easy to clean, perfect for reading, bedside-table-free, emanating

Top
ABA 'Shelf Life', designed for the Atoll Hotel, Germany, 2000. This replaced the usual set-pieces of hotel furniture with one continuous 7-metre structure cantilevered from the wall.

Middle
ABA 'Let There Be Light', designed for the Atoll Hotel. A bed, with a wall-mounted, self-illuminating headboard.

Bottom
ABA bar in the Atoll Hotel. The concave copper walls that enclose the conference room become freestanding screens/bench supports in the lobby bar.

friendliness and a pretty good substitute for someone to go to bed with. The headboard, part wall, part bed, part light, and the wall unit, part wall, part bench, part adventure playground, both turn on when the hotel-room door is opened. But being structural wall dependent and slightly 'dangerous', these pieces are not destined for the commercial furniture market.

Other spaces in the hotel are places defined by and for built-in furniture. The concave copper walls that enclose the conference room become freestanding screens/bench supports in the lobby bar. The restaurant, elevated on a timber platform like a dock above water, is pierced by glass cylinders holding banquettes and is framed by long benches covered in white leatherette like yachts in the Med. The giant communal starfish -like table in the Bistro (fitting the most people into the smallest circular space) gets total strangers to sit opposite each other (like the finger-shaped eating counters of the Greyhound Bus diners of my youth). This attenuated blob has been made into the hotel's logo – a cross -fertilisation of memory, metaphor and space -saving socialising furniture with graphic design.

VXO, Transgressive design and Domestic Life

The VXO house, a large residential project in North London by ABA, has been a field for assimilating architecture, art, built-in furniture and landscape. Here there has been an intentional blurring of boundaries between all of these subjects, an opportunity to reassign assumed roles. The project began as a two -storey front extension to a 1960s house and a combined vertical and horizontal opening of the house interior. The new glass-enclosed foyer of the extension allows the 'solid' volume of the bedrooms above to appear as hovering over an outdoor terrace, supported by one structural 'V'. The foyer was conceived as part of the landscape, and elements within the foyer as vertical screens delineating that landscape. Therefore a translucent, sometimes vibrating screen suspended from the first floor is also the stair – a bent timber plank held by walls of rigid stainless steel mesh. Art replaces 'architectural

material' in the long freestanding wall that screens the hall closet and guest toilet. Turner Prize shortlisted artist Simon Patterson's installation with its reinterpreted 1960s wiring diagram ('Ohm Sweet Ohm') disguises a door and extends into the garden, art framing the public and screening the private landscape.

Other elements in the house are backdrop furniture – a 3-metre long a/v unit is a three-dimensional tower of painted or upholstered grey cubes (furniture disappears into the background). A desk is made from two vertical layers peeling off the wall to form a horizontal sandwich space that eats unwanted cables (the walls become the desk); a door to a bedroom is formed from a wall of cupboards where one cupboard is 'pushed in' for the room entrance (the closet becomes the architecture). In the garden X-Pavilion (gym/guest-house) by ABA the floor bends vertically to form a wall embedded with doors to service spaces. At the property entrance the new carport consists of a timber roof supported by two stainless steel 'picture frames' (which the cars must drive through) and a structural 'O' that frames the landscape beyond. In this project a cross-referencing between landscape, art, structure and furniture aims to create a 'domestic campus' of transgressive yet sensory architecture. The challenge now must be to transplant this notion of trans-operational design out of the context of the rarefied 'one-off' and into the realm of the commercial, the affordable, the sociopolitical and the mass-produced. △

Above left
In the garden X-Pavilion (gym/guest house) of the VXO House, the floor bends vertically to form a wall embedded with doors to service spaces

Above right
ABA's design for 'Shelf Life' style seating as street furniture for public space – taking the rarefied 'one-off' and putting it in a context that is accessible and affordable.

Below
Allsort desk, VXO House.

Home/Furnishings

Best known for their winning entry in the international competition for disaster relief housing in Kosovo, New York-based practice **Gans & Jelacic** are accustomed to applying their architectural, industrial and product-design skills at many different scales, ranging from mass housing to shelter and furniture design. This is exemplified by one of their most recent designs, Workbox (Δ, vol 71, no 6) in which a school desk is transformed into a foldout enclosure or mini-building structure. Here Gans & Jelacic have fully tested the parameters of furniture and architecture by exploring the idea of 'home/ furnishings' in their own work and also in that of three emerging US practices – AC2, Ascher-Barnstone and R+D Design.

Below
Afghani woman in Burkha.

In the newspaper photos, the blue Burkha glides down the street, a bell-shaped tent bound to the body within only at the crown. Our Western eyes see it as the blackout cover of a birdcage or a form of mobile house arrest, but, for the willing wearer, it is a tool in the domestication of urban space. Take, for example, contemporary Algerian women of Brussels who did not wear veils in Algiers but have adopted them as a matter of comfort and privacy, a drapery drawn across their window to the boulevard of a new and strange city. As with these garments, interior furnishings when dislocated to the exterior take on the characteristics of architecture and, conversely, architectural objects when internalised become furnishing. The projects that follow by our own office and by three colleagues whom we admire, explore transpositions of location, material, scale and use between architecture and furniture.

Gans & Jelacic

'Roy's Shower'
Apartment Renovation
Riverside Drive
New York City
1991–97

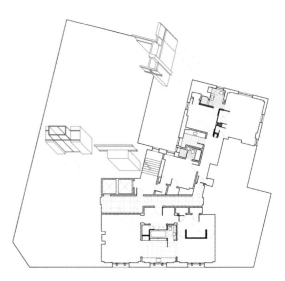

Deborah Gans and Matthew Jelacic: From a small office near the pinnacle of the Empire State Building in New York, Deborah Gans and Matthew Jelacic work on a diverse range of projects that encompass industrial, exhibition and graphic design, as well as architecture. An ongoing project is their research into alternative forms of housing. They have designed with Marguerite McGoldrick a transitional housing system for CommonGround Community, which was exhibited at the Van Alen Institute for Public Architecture in New York City. Their disaster relief housing for Kosovo won an international competition sponsored by USAID, Architecture for Humanity, and WarChild; a subsequent grant for development has been awarded by the KeepWalking Fund of Johnny Walker. Their patented 'next generation school desk', or Workbox, is now in production.

A while ago, we completed a small interior furnishing that has become a kind of obsessive reference and an ideogram for us under the shorthand designation of 'Roy's Shower'. The original 1908 grand apartments of Roy's building were summarily butchered after the Crash of 1929 such that Roy occupied an original dining room, living room and a library into which a kitchen and bath had been inserted. We understood his brief to redo the kitchen as his desire to restore the pre-Depression grandeur, the library window and the enfilade of movement and view along the river – without increasing the square footage. We understood that he wanted to inhabit the apartment both according to the mores of 1908 when space was luxurious because cooking and bodily functions were hidden away, and according to current desires for bathrooms and kitchens as elegant and public as the former library.

In response we decided to put the bathroom in a box and move it to the foyer. This box is really a small Meisan house; a solid-section steel and glass enclosure of four structural posts, with cantilevered roof girders, and secondary beams hung from the cantilevers. It stands independent of the apartment with its own little footings submerged in the floor slab, and its roof structure opening on to the sky of a new skylight.

In its displacement from building to shower, the structure takes on the qualities of interior furnishing. Its glass enclosure is a translucent shade between foyer and library window; its pantry and bathroom walls are wood panelling hung beneath the architectural detail of cornices; its uprights are shelving.

There are three principles condensed within the ideogram of the shower:
1. It is a freestanding, self-supporting object and enclosure nested within an existing shell. It does not disturb the shell it touches.
2. This nested structure is required by the dysfunction of the existing shell. The original rooms need the new furnishing in order to work as an apartment.
3. The added element is hyper-programmed: armoire, pantry, refrigerator, shelving unit, window shade. It has many accessible sides that can independently respond to their adjacencies with new patterns of use.

There is a two-part coda to this story in which Roy's shower is displaced, materially translated and transformed as Roy and his wife Ann migrate within the space of the building. To house their new child, we translated the shower in wood, opening one side to make a crèche. Unable to acquire an adjacent unit, they bought the remote piece of the original apartment, gave away the crèche, and constructed another, double-sided, multi-purpose armoire of wood that winds its away around the existing structure. For now, they walk along the common building corridor between their living rooms and bedrooms as if between houses on a boulevard.

Credits: Deborah Gans, Matthew Jelacic, Brian McGrath and Anthony Webster (structural engineer).

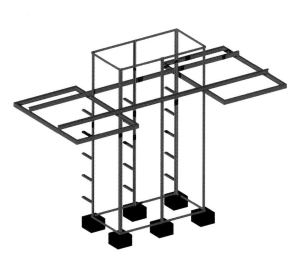

Opposite top right
Plan of the two parts of the
1908 apartment owned by
Roy and the corridor between.
The three phases of renovation
are shown simultaneously in
axonometric.

Opposite top left
Roy's Shower detail view.

Top left
Shower Interior.

Middle
Roy's Shower from the former
library, now a kitchen.
The pantry and refrigerator
are to the right of the shower,
the bathroom to the left.
The glass shelves rest on
steel c-sections welded
to the columns.

Top right
Ideogram.

Bottom left
Foyer shot. The original
foyer view to the river
through the mirror on
the door to the dining
room was reconstructed.

Bottom right
Roy's Shower from foyer:
Enhanced by its skylight,
the shower enclosure allows
light from the original library
window to extend to the foyer.

Gans & Jelacic

Disaster Relief Housing for Kosovo, 1999–

Winning design for the competition sponsored by Architecture for Humanity. Exhibited at RIBA, London, IFA, Paris, Van Alen Institute, New York. Gans & Jelacic were recently awarded a grant from the KeepWalking Fund of Johnny Walker to develop this project in prototype. Disassembled into modular panels and stacked and tied for shipping, the two boxes have a total volume of 1130 millimetres square by 1100 millimetres high. The palettes form a protective top and bottom for the panels stacked between. The cistern barrel holds the steel brackets, hardware, miscellaneous components and tools for the eventual resurrection of the permanent house. Twenty emergency shelters fit in a standard 20-foot shipping container. It is estimated that a team of four can erect the emergency shelter in six hours using a single wrench.

Opposite above right
Shelter in a Camp Situation. The left box is the privy clad with translucent fibreglass and solid panels insulated with local materials such as straw. The box to the right is the kitchen with metal cooking surfaces and cladding to conduct heat, and an integral cistern that also serves as a shower from the opposite side. The sleeping area between the boxes is protected with a photovoltaic tarpaulin the energy of which is stored in a battery that powers the TV – the most universally requested of appliances.

Opposite above left and below right
Shelter Within the Eventual Home. Erected on the site of a damaged house, the boxes are configured according to household patterns, further domesticated with the unrolling of possessions and extended with beams which will serve for the construction of the permanent house around it.

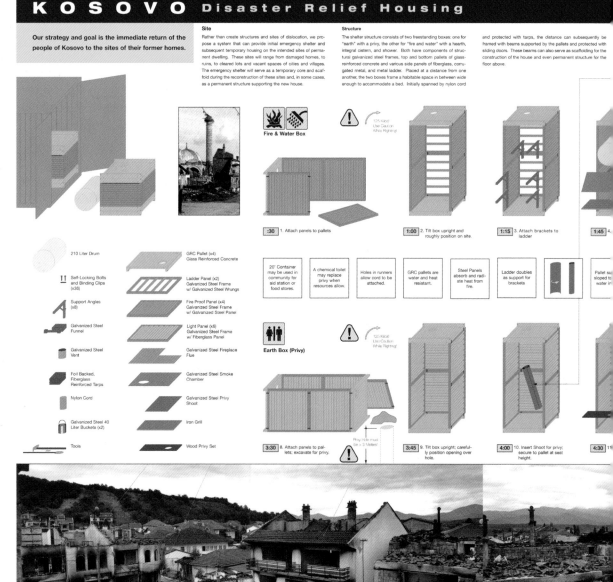

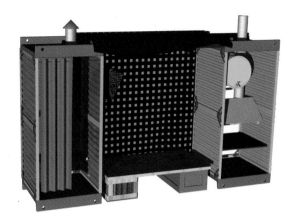

Disassembled into modular panels and stacked and tied for shipping, the two boxes have a total volume of 1130 mm square by 1100 mm high. The palettes form a protective top and bottom for the panels and various sheets of metal stacked between. The cistern barrel holds the steel brackets, hardware, miscellaneous components, and tools for the eventual resurrection of the permanent house. Twenty emergency shelters fit in a standard twenty foot shipping container.

Hoisted from truck via the grips provided on the palettes and placed on the site, we estimate a team of four can erect the emergency shelter in less than six hours. The drawings below illustrate the step-by-step assembly.

| 2:00 | 5. Attach hoses with stop-cocks to drum | 2:15 | 6. Attach brackets for shower enclosure. | 2:30 | 7. Use nylon cord to attach tarp for shower enclosure. |

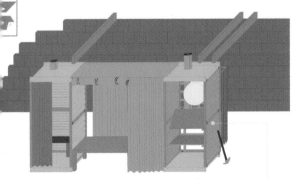

| 5:00 | 12. Use nylon cord to suspend tarp for privacy. | >6:00 | 13. Use nylon cord to suspend tarps for enclosure between boxes. |

In our project for disaster relief housing, the displacement of the interior is not metaphoric. According to the competition brief which was the basis for our proposal, these shelters for refugee camps had to be erected very quickly – in as little as 48 hours – from a limited amount of material, but remain standing for as long as two years. Rather than create structures and sites of dislocation, our strategy was the immediate return of the people to the sites of their former homes. We proposed a system that could provide initial shelter in a camp situation but then subsequent housing on the sites of permanent dwelling, whether damaged homes, ruins, or the cleared lots of cities and villages.

The emergency shelter consists of two freestanding steel-framed boxes with top and bottom pallets of glass-reinforced concrete and various infill panels such as fibreglass, metal and insulating straw. One is furnished as a privy, the other as a kitchen with integral cistern and shower. Placed at a distance from one another, they frame a habitable space wide enough to accommodate a bed. Initially spanned by nylon cord and protected with curtains of photovoltaic tarpaulin, the distance can be subsequently framed with beams so that the shelter becomes a core and a scaffold for the construction of a house around it. As self-supporting, multi-directional, hyper-programmed, inhabited objects that will (eventually) nest within the larger architectural shell they restore, these boxes are Roy's Shower.

AC2

Sunny Bates Associates,
New York City, 2000–01

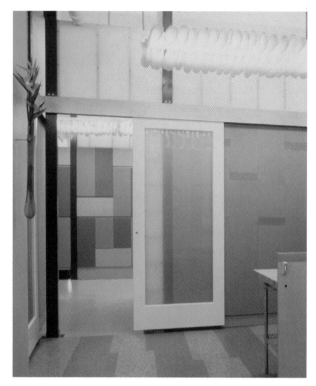

AC2 Studio was established in 1997 in New York City by Anthony Caradonna and Anita Cooney. It is an interdisciplinary design practice, which is engaged in architectural projects as well as the design of interiors, furniture, lighting and textile works. Both teach at Pratt Institute where Anthony Caradonna is currently Chair of the Undergraduate Architecture Department. Anita Cooney was formerly Associate Chair.

The alliance of the textile arts, home furnishings and architecture have their theoretical formulation in Gottfried Semper who tells us that architecture began as the carpets hung from the frame of the nomadic tent. The textile nature of the wall is lost, he submitted, for it is inscribed in the patterning of brick or mosaic and, one might continue, in the translucent marble of the Meisian screen, or in the weaving of wood and the stitching of felt in the projects which follow.

AC2's offices for Sunny Bates capitalise on the Semperian confusion of textile and architecture and the play among wall, carpet, floor drapery, covering and cushion that it allows. The range of the textile art is exuberantly present in the manipulations of draping, folding, stuffing, stitching and creasing, and also in the variable qualities of the materials themselves – wool felt, velvet, knits, short pile – all of which give a perceptual depth within a quite small dimension of surface. The walls are upholstered, the light fixtures draped, the linoleum colours seamed and so forth so that the entire space is stitched together like a quilt. Conversely, the scale of the fabric patch alludes to architectural tiling, which is then literally present in the linoleum floor and ceramic bathroom surface. The framework supporting the textile panels has bypassing members in x-y-z directions as if the tent structure and surface were exploded slightly to fit the space.

UM Felt Baffle, 1999

Opposite top left
Plan of the offices of Sunny
Bates Associates. A zone of
break-out rooms or small
conference rooms serving the
perimeter offices runs down
the centre of the space
creating intermittent cross-
axes of colour and layers of
surface that expand the sense
of depth.

Opposite top right
View through break-out room
in offices. Part of the pleasure
of the textile in relation to the
spatial organisation of the plan
is the view created through
different zones of colour and
pattern. The centre rooms
borrow natural light through
transoms allowing the textiles
a rich appearance.

Opposite bottom
Corridor in Sunny Bates
Associates. The material
palette of the job has an
economy as well as an
aesthetic such that the office
construction was $45 a square
foot. The framing is fibreglass,
which has cost savings in
material and labour in that it is
light, easy to handle and drill.
The detailing of the beams and
columns as separate planes
minimised cuts and joints while
articulating the idea of the
exploded frame. The apparent
endless variety of pattern is
actually achieved through a
systematised and repetitive use
of a 2-foot module of Homosote
panels disguised with fabric
and colour.

Right
UM Light: The patented UM
light baffle of polyester felt
placed over a standard
fluorescent (SP30 lamp) light
softens the harsh glare of bare
tubes, absorbs ambient noise,
and transforms the raw
industrial fixture into a softly
glowing silhouette of
undulating curved surfaces. A
variety of shapes are produced
from a number of simple
template patterns. The felt is
pre-cut to fit and fold easily
over standard lengths of
fluorescent lighting tubes, then
mounted on a mediating plastic
sleeve that separates the felt
from the bare bulb. Regularly
spaced holes in the felt allow
the plastic sleeve to safely
support and shape the felt into
various geometric patterns.

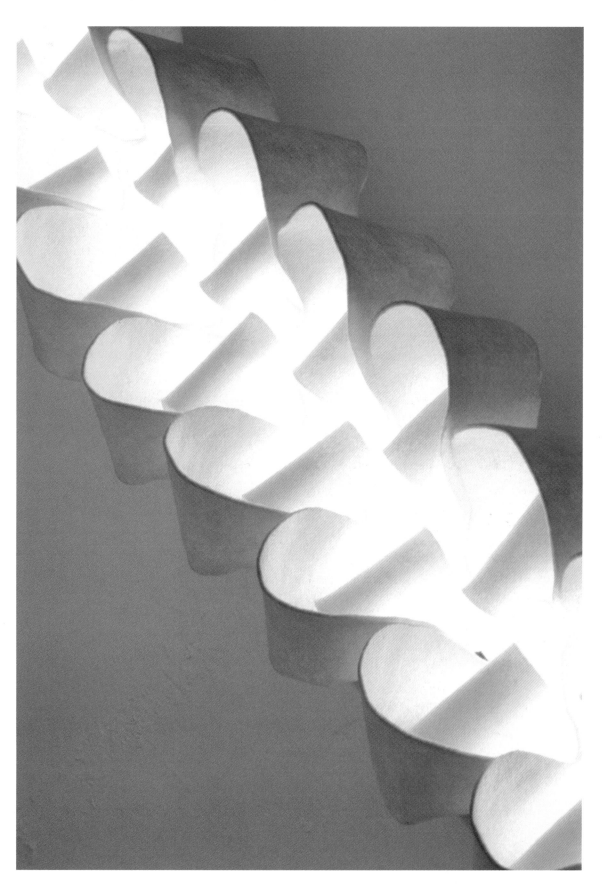

Ascher-Barnstone

Indiana Sukkot Project, Muncie, Indiana, 1997
Wall Studies, Washington State University School of Architecture, 2001

Ascher/Barnstone
Deborah Ascher Barnstone and Robert Barnstone have offices in
Pullman, Washington, Rossland British Columbia, and Serifos, Greece.
Both are currently professors in architecture at Washington State
University, Pullman. Ascher Barnstone is completing her PhD at the
Technical University in Delft on issues of transparency. Robert Barnstone
is continuing to explore plastic form-making through art architecture. He
has shown his work at Socrates Sculpture Park in New York, at Roger
Williams Park in Providence Rhode Island, in the new sculpture park in
Bridgeport, Connecticut, at Exit Art Gallery in Cologne, Germany, and in
galleries in Boston and San Francisco.

Right
Robert Barnstone, The Wall
Between – Shelter Vessel.
Layers of wood are woven
around framing elements in
a complex stereotomic
construction with reference to
structures found in nomadic
African societies and tropical
architectures in general.

Top far right
Ascher-Barnstone, Indiana
Sukkot. The Sukkah is built
of wood indigenous to Indiana.
The entire structure is in
sections small enough for
assembly by two people in a
couple of hours. It is raised
off the ground on two large
wooden beams so that it
appears to hover or float, as
an expression of its nomadic
and temporary nature. The
benches and suspended table
are designed to fold up and
leave the space free. On one
face is a shelving unit in which
ritual objects can be stored.

Middle far right
Robert Barnstone and
students from Washington
State University School of
Architecture, Wall Studies.
Students were asked to design
an 8-foot square wall that
could be assembled with other
walls in a variety of
configurations to make spaces
for contemplation. Louisiana
Pacific donated the base
materials, some of which were
then used in the manufacture
of the composite plastic wood
by the University's Wood
Products Engineering
Laboratories. This Wall project
was designed and built by WSU
student Todd Garrett in spring
2001.

Bottom far right
The benches and suspended
table are designed to fold up
and leave the space free. On
one face is a shelving unit in
which ritual objects can be
stored.

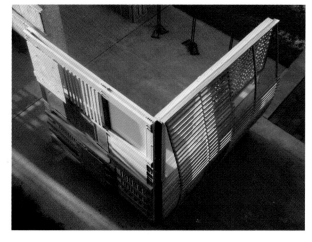

The ancient Succoth was a tent erected in the
fields for a harvest holiday and it carries that
lineage in its contemporary interpretation by
Ascher-Barnstone. The enclosing surfaces are
an open weave of wood, interlaced with corn
husks on the roof that bring to mind the alliance
of textiles and baskets. The table for the ritual
feast is consciously oversized to fill, if not
overwhelm the space as a sign of nature's
bounty. The realised intention of the architects
was to join the shelter and its furniture as a
single vessel for the harvest.

While the bare glass curtain wall may well
be both Semper's legacy and nightmare, it has
engendered its own layered dressing of
Venetian blind, pull shades, plastic sheeting,
curtains and drapes to control light, heat, cold,
view and self-exposure. Robert Barnstone and
his students at Washington State University play
with the domestication and dressing of the
glass wall by translating it into the gritty
materials of sheathed construction like
Homosote, and unfinished ply, and yet
simulating some of the delicacy associated with
textile. In his own sculptural Shelter Vessel, the
wall and its curtain are further conflated in a
screen of great plasticity.

R+D

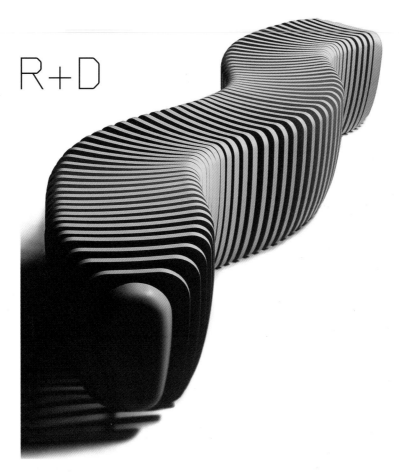

Sophie Demenge and Michael Ryan are the founders and designers of R+D Design, a New York-based company specialising in furniture, ceramics, lighting and accessories. Their ongoing mission and delight is to provide innovative, high-quality design for the home and office.

Above
Worm Bench designed by Michael Ryan. Each segment of the bench is independently attached to the steel-rod spine so that the entire curve is easily reconfigured. The bench pictured is 9 feet in length but its potential extension is endless.

Middle
Sophie Demenge, Corian Tables, 2000. Corian top on steel base.

Bottom
Michael Ryan and Sophie Demenge, stained plywood screen designed for New York furniture store The Apartment, 2000.

Plastic – as both material and the eponymous quality – describes many of the *au courant* transfers between furnishings and architecture. Entire buildings mimic the profiles of the Panton Chair while curtain walls are fabricated from plexi-glass formerly relegated to the coffee table. (The small extruded sections of the Barnstone students' screen are a new hybrid of plastic and recycled wood currently in development at the Wood Products Materials Laboratory at Washington State University. Amoebae that eat wood and excrete plastic as a by-product will eventually produce the material.)

Industrial designers R+D have taken the tradition of furniture's plasticity and brought it to bear on architectural materials and sizes, as with their enormous Worm Bench of LDF vertebrae along a steel-rod spine, and their Corian trays and tables. For quality control, Dupont, the manufacturer of Corian, limits the material's large-scale use to the netherworld between architecture and furniture that is the kitchen/bathroom countertop; but R+D wrest it from the threat of banality in their tables impressed with the dishware usually placed upon it. They have then transferred the formal qualities of these smallest of daily objects to a monumental plywood screen as part of the endless and pleasurable translation between architecture and furniture. ⌂

Light.
Knob.
Felt.
Things:
A Chat
with
Tom
Emerson
of 6A
about
'the
World
of Stuff'

Looking beyond the myths and conventions of the Modernist project, **Tom Emerson** of London-based design practice 6A questions the relevance of 'total architecture'. Through a discussion of his own work and the photographs of Richard Wentworth, he explained to Edwin Heathcote how designed items in a real rather than a removed context should attempt to engage with rather than shun their surroundings.

Space begins on the page. That, at least, is how Georges Perec began his book *Species of Spaces*: 'This is how space begins, with words only, signs traced on the blank pages.... Is the Aleph, that place in Borges from which the entire world is visible simultaneously, anything other than an alphabet?'[1]

And it was Perec who got us talking. I was enthusing to Tom Emerson from 6A about the author's *Life: A User's Manual*, he to me about *Species of Spaces*. Emerson, it transpired, wrote his dissertation on Perec, and his early work as a student exploited the link which Perec points out between words and space, between objects, spaces and life.[2]

'My interest is less to do with furniture and more to do with things in general, the relationship between objects and architecture. Certainly during the Modernist era furniture has been to complete an architectural set-piece. A lot of those items were designed for a specific project and were to do with filling in a gap so that when it came to photographing the spaces, they were furnished with these things to complete a manifesto or polemic.

My interest is less to do with furniture and more to do with things in general, the relationship between objects and architecture.

'I'm not interested in designing furniture for a project; what I'm doing in an architectural work is to import things, although we do some fitted furniture. I quite like it when it gets contaminated by other stuff, not necessarily part of the world of design or conscious aesthetics, it's more relaxed. But then I'm very interested in things, in objects and their relationship to architecture.'

In that case, I asked, if we take Corb loungers or Mies chairs which become kind of cliches, what is the difference between things and these 'classic designs'?

'Mies or Corb chairs become kind of icons, representations of a bigger idea. I'm interested in the sometimes contradictory messages you receive when you experience a piece of architecture through objects, furniture or things. The kind of furniture you're talking about is an extension of the architecture and originates from the same architectural context. It then gets removed from that context and then starts representing that polemic. For me things don't evoke a particular kind of architecture. The way

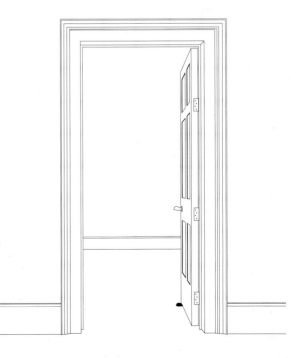

Opposite
6A, light, 2001 – hardly more than a disc above a bare light bulb. Emerson stripped down the design to a mere light bulb and then added the disc to make clear that its nakedness was 'intentional'.

Top left
The 6a team. Left to right: Steph Macdonald, Tom Emerson and Lee Marsden.

Right top and bottom
6A, door knob designed for Izé, 2001. Rather than developing other designs or prototypes, Emerson took a sideways approach to the knob's design. Starting to consider the context in which it was used – 'the world of doors, which are to do with opening and closing' – he came up with the idea of a knob that is also a door wedge.

Standard | at 20°C   BS. 4572

1   2   3   4   5   6   7   8   9   10   11   12   13   14   15   16

JAN   FEB   MAR   APR   MAY   JUN

I conceive them and think about them isn't in terms of a particular space but in terms of autonomy – I don't want to try to second-guess or impose anything on to the context into which they'll be placed. I guess there's also a linguistic interest there, about the object as a sign as well as itself. In my mind these are autonomous things and if there is, it's a historical or linguistic context. For the door knob I've drawn a Georgian panelled door, which is rather to place it into the world; the panelled door becomes a kind of shorthand for "door".

'In the case of the light, it's been stripped back so far that it would be almost pointless to prescribe a context. I find it quite a difficult object to talk about because really, it's so simple, there's not much to say. People either immediately like it or they don't.'

So how did the lamp come about?

'I never sat down to design a light. I'd been frustrated for a while trying to specify something and I think in drawings I just used a naked light-bulb. And I quite liked that. But afterwards it seemed one tiny step too far. It needed something to make it look intentional; what can you add to a light bulb and flex to make that seem like an intentional gesture. So I just drew this disc, got a piece of cardboard, covered in foil and made a hole in it. It's something which is hardly there.'

I'd liked the light so much that I approached Tom to design a door handle. I asked him to explain the ideas embodied in the design he returned with:

'The door-knob was much more conscious. The background is that I'd been very interested in the relationship between things and architecture, the city, particularly in Richard Wentworth's photography. Suddenly you realise that a seemingly infinite number of things surround us but actually when brought together in certain situations maintain quite curious relationships, often ones well outside their intended use. His photograph of a teaspoon holding open a sash window.'

I mention Neil Cummings's photo of the polypropylene chairs being used to reserve a city parking space which he took for the essay in this book – 'Exactly'.

'When you asked us to think about a door handle, I remember sitting down one evening at home and sketching lots of shapes, and then I looked at a catalogue to see which ones had been done already and then I just got frustrated with the whole process. I didn't want to do another shape. If it was going to be interesting I wanted to do a bit more and I started thinking maybe the handle or knob should be quite straightforward and that maybe it was to do with its relationship with other objects, other things around the world of doors which are to do with opening and closing. That's when the idea of the wedge emerged and the relationship with the object holding the

door open, whether that be sticks, bits of paper or even chairs, whatever, and I suddenly thought perhaps the two could become one object that separates when it needs to but then comes back together. It was something about making marriages between apparently disconnected objects. The knob has a kind of natural curvature and a section sliced off is the right shape.'

If the light and knob take care of ceilings and doors, we're still left with the floors. 6A's most complete engagement with the interior has been in the stores for fashion retailer oki-ni. With an unusual retailing strategy of displaying in a shop but ordering (the special versions of otherwise mass-produced garments) online, the client required an unusual shop-fit. What 6a gave them was a branding through furniture and display technique. Rather than slick shelving or vitrines, clothes are displayed on piles of felt. The distinctive semi-naked lights hang sparsely above the displayed items giving an entirely different lighting effect to the traditional overkill of high-tech high-street super-commercial artificial daylight. To complement these felt stands the practice developed felt-covered furniture, of which the fuzzy chairs are the most characteristic.

'I first saw felt used this way in a Beuys installation, felt and fat and that kind of thing. I also saw the preparations for a show at the Royal Academy where paintings were being placed on the floor below their final positions and were supported on lumps of felt and

timber. These felt blocks were such beautiful things, Joseph Beuys couldn't have done them better. When we did the competition for oki-ni, they were talking about natural materials and so on, and we saw our chance. The other thing about these things is that they can increase or decrease in size according to the context without the design changing. For the chairs we wanted to carry the felt through. The displays so far had been about trying to get away from the world of the shop rack, the endless supplies of similar goods.'

So, they got a standard-looking chair and clad it in felt, clothed it almost in the shop's corporate image.

'When you place it [the garment] on a chair it makes it more particular, more domestic almost. It also reinforces the idea that it's more of an installation, that it's all very light and could just be taken away at any point. That's why furniture seemed to be the right thing to do, just placing these things lightly. But of course, their brand identity is in the felt.'

So, I suggest, the furniture has become the corporate image?

'Yes, and they were quite particular about where they spent their money, rather than a huge ad campaign they invested it in the store.'

So what, I asked Tom, is the relationship between architecture and furniture?

'Certainly during the 20th century the Modernist project sort of puts architecture into its own little world; you design buildings expecting people to get some kind of pure architectural sensation from it. I think since then though cities have become so messy that every architectural experience is preceded and then is followed by a world of stuff, and I find that this idea that you can have this slightly sacred experience of architecture a bit romantic and naive. You have to deal with this fact that there's always stuff, whether it be literally in front of you or just in your memory.'

In that case, I asked, does stuff actually need to be designed? It seems that what we're talking about here is a kind of anti-design, a rebellion against the plastic gee-gaws of Alessi or the ubiquity of the space-blob which breeds in the windows of the world's ever-converging design stores. We're talking about the world of the real, a world where objects are made to improvise to participate because of secondary characteristics, their weight perhaps, or their strength. We're talking about chairs reserving parking spaces, mugs used as paperweights and so on. Is it possible for your objects to participate in this world recorded by Richard Wentworth and Neil Cummings?

'Not literally, and I don't think you can because the sort of world they're talking about is about people being resourceful and inventive beyond what is intended and suggested by the object. But what I'd like it to do is to have a certain level of legibility so that it does offer that potential; the opposite is the idea of the i-mac where a

whole world gets wrapped up in an ergonomic plastic bubble which is completely impenetrable as an object you can't participate with – if the shell cracks, that's it. I hope our objects are a little more robust, both physically and literally. I hope our work can make explicit certain relationships between things which are always present. What I would hope is that, certainly with the door knob, suddenly it puts lots of other objects under suspicion. You suddenly become aware that there are many things in the material world which are related. We spoke about the door knob and someone using it without ever realising that there was a wedge in it, just thinking it's a soft bit underneath. These things do make visible certain things about our material world.'

So is your interest in design literal or practical? (Big pause.)

'It is literal to the extent that I'm more interested in a world-view of objects rather than the technocratic view, but having said that I couldn't build it without having an intense interest in the practice of it. You have to understand the real context in which these things exist.'

Meaning and making, I suggest?

'The making is at the heart of the meaning and I don't intend that in the Modernist sense of form following function. If anything I think form follows dysfunction, things become much more honest if

they are broken and get repaired. But I think that the process is critical, not just in the physical sense but in the economic and cultural sense. The industrial context and the processes through which things are made, and the consumer-based culture of which these things are going to become a part, are equally important.

'The way these things are made, that kind of industrial and social context, as well as the more consumer-based culture, the environment which these things are going to join, a culture which is bursting with things, is just as important.

'The relationship I have to all these designs is quite weird. I always feel a little concerned by the proximity to the art object. I haven't completely resolved that. Although I don't lose any sleep over it, I'm not too worried about exactly how something is read.'

Reading things? That brings us back to Perec. In his essay 'Notes concerning the objects that are on my work-table'[3] he fastidiously lists the items he has cluttered around himself. It is the blend of the useless and the useful, the almost forensic approach to listing and the profound portrait of life which emerges from the world of stuff which makes Perec's work so readable and so fascinating to architects. Tom Emerson's objects inhabit this world of things between the useful, the funny and the quotidian. ⚙

Tom Emerson's door knob and light are available from Izé. For more details see retail listing at the back of the issue.

Footnotes
1. Georges Perec, *Species of Spaces and Other Pieces*, Penguin (London), 1997, p 13.
2. Tom Emerson's work on Perec is featured in a book compiled by Eric Parry and Peter Carl, *On Certain Possibilities for the Irrational Embellishment of a Town*, Black Dog (Cambridge), 2000.
3. Georges Perec, op cit, pp 144–47.

Superlegible Furniture or 'We like junk'

PLANT Architect Inc is a Toronto-based architecture and design practice led by Chris Pommer, Lisa Rapoport and Mary Tremain. It works on landscape design and master-planning projects in Canada and the US, as well as architectural design, renovations, furniture and graphics. Producing projects at almost every scale, it consistently engages with issues concerning the environment. PLANT's Superlegible Furniture designs were the result of a commission by the Toronto Design Exchange to address sustainability in furniture design.

We like places and things that are ignored or scorned, but that have unnoticed qualities that can be hidden delights.

Much of our experimentation has been about creating a dialogue between the viewer and the landscape. Our approach does not stem from an overarching ecological agenda; rather, it is a by-product of our interest in the traces that our culture leaves on the land. Our aim is to heighten people's awareness of their environment: we believe people must first recognise and be engaged with their environment before they will take a role in sustaining it. We often use 'furniture' as a physical container for both material and cultural content in the landscape – it engages the body directly, and encourages lingering.

With Superlegible Furniture, we had an opportunity to point out a popular misconception about our waste-management infrastructure, while positing one approach to dealing with the stuff of our daily lives. This prototype furniture is one of four commissions by the Toronto Design Exchange 'to foster dialogue and new critical thinking in the field of sustainable furniture' for the exhibit 'New Landscape: Design Transforms Canadian Furniture'.

Reducing waste materials – one aspect of sustainability – means adjusting our attitudes to consumption and waste altogether. We propose harvesting available discarded material, and treating it instead as raw material. The city is our natural resource. With more of our waste kept around us in a closed system, we will be more aware of the materials that we feel all too comfortable throwing out, and, perhaps, we will be less willing to just 'toss it in the bin'.

The furniture is made from newspaper: catching a ubiquitous, recyclable and generally-viewed-as-trash material, midstream in its recycling life, and extending that life. Though the newspaper is recyclable, it often fills up warehouses for far too long, waiting for a buyer.

The furniture pairs two lifespan concepts. The containers are permanent heirlooms, and easily disassembled: solid wood and leather, both sustainable materials if supply is managed appropriately. The filling – rolls of newspapers – is expendable and replaceable. When the newspaper is spent, it can return to the

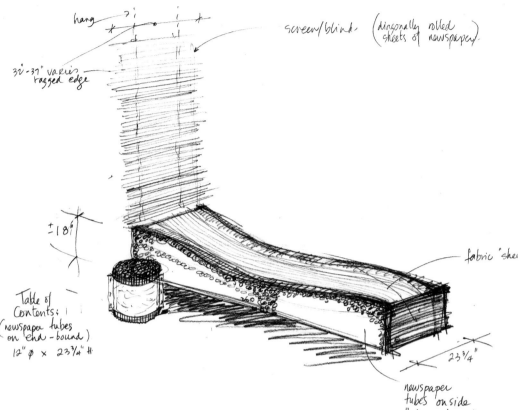

hang

screen/blind. (diagonally rolled sheets of newspaper).

32"-37" varies ragged edge

± 18"

Table of Contents: (newspaper tubes on end - bound) 12" ∅ × 23¾" H.

fabric "she

23¾"

newspaper tubes on side "air-cushioned" length = 6'-6"

domestic recycling box and continue on its previous recycling path.

We explored the structural and aesthetic possibilities of newspaper – using it in multiples, dyeing it, and transforming it from a weak, transitory and everyday reading object into a textured, cellular structure of typographic and image fragments.

Seven-hundred single-sheet (double page) rolls with 13-millimetre diameter hollow centres are tightly wrapped in a leather band to form the stool. The seemingly insubstantial edge of the newspaper is used in compression to create a light, stiff and stable ensemble.

Fourteen-hundred four-sheet (double page) rolls with 11-millimetre diameter hollow centres are loosely stacked in a demountable maple frame with a leather runner blanket on top to form the chaise longue. Like a cushion, the stack of loose rolls has a spring-like resilience and adjusts to the body. The rolls are lightly glued with wheat wallpaper paste. Rolling could be automated or produced by cottage industry. A do-it-yourself repair kit would include a dowel and some powdered paste. ⊅

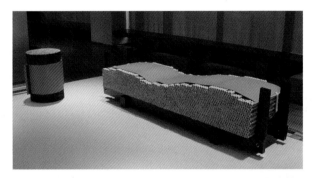

Opposite
Chris Pommer, Lisa Rapoport and Mary Tremain of PLANT Architect Inc.

Above
Overall sketch of Superlegible Furniture.

Right
Superlegible Furniture exhibited at the 'New Landscape: Design Transforms Canadian Furniture' at the Toronto Design Exchange.

Item Design Laboratory
Love Seats for Virginia Woolf and Lady Furniture

Item Design Laboratory, Love Seats and Lady Furniture on exhibition at A: D/B Project Space in Fort Greene, Brooklyn, February 2002.

A kind of biography through architecture, Love Seats and Lady Furniture are a unique departure. Representing both a new transmission or transmutation of the biographic genre, the seats pose a whole new range of subject and form-giving possibilities for furniture-design. They reflect Annie Coggan and Caleb Crawford of Item Design Laboratory's interest in architecture as a storytelling mechanism and the idea that furniture holds layers of history and cultural content. The primary question in Love Seats is: can history have a narrative content? The formal investigation resides in the particular context of their subject matter, thus they are presented as diagrams or gestures of the relationship between the individuals in the Bloomsbury set.

The seats chart the particular shift that has taken place in Coggan and Crawford's practice and are in this way an important expression of the steady evolution that is taking place in the relationship between furniture and architecture. Conceived by artist/designer Annie Coggan, they were realised in collaboration with Caleb Crawford, as part of the partner's Item Design Laboratory project. IDL was set up in 1993 as the experimental arm of their architectural practice, Coggan + Crawford, as a means of exploring toy design, furniture prototypes and theatrical space design to the side of their main architectural output. Increasingly, however, the larger proportion of Coggan + Crawford's work has been given over to custom-designed furniture. This has motivated Coggan + Crawford to provide a renewed focus to Item Design Laboratory's work. With Love Seats and Lady Furniture providing the prototype for biographical furniture, IDL aims to design furniture for clients who wish to have their own qualities uniquely expressed and developed in the form or programme of their particular piece. ⌂

Ali Tayar
Furniture as Structure

Having worked with wide-span aeroplane hangars, on tensile structures with the firm FTL and on glass walls with James Carpenter, Ali Tayar with his New York-based practice Parallel Design Partnership has shifted their interest to furniture. **Jayne Merkel** describes how Tayar is converting structural reasoning to table legs and shelf units.

'Most of the work we have produced in the last ten years is furniture and objects but to me they are architectural constructions. I view them as small buildings.' Ali Tayar began a lecture in the prestigious Emerging Architects series at the Architectural League of New York this March. The table projected in front of the audience, at many times its size, did indeed look like a baby Hagia Sophia or, as he suggested, Eero Saarinen's concrete-shelled Kresge Auditorium. Four plywood shells intersect to form a cross-vault supporting a round glass table top.

'I tried to use structural reasoning down to the tabs on the feet', Tayar explained as he showed a detail of the splay at the base of the leg. 'The logic is that better structural sense makes better aesthetic sense.'

This soft-spoken, Turkish-born, New York architect attributes his way of thinking to his training at the University of Stuttgart and at the Massachusetts Institute of Technology. When he got out of school, he worked on wide-span airplane hangars with Lev Zetlin, on tensile structures with FTL, and on James Carpenter's pioneering glass walls.

Soon after founding the Parallel Design Partnership in 1992, Tayar created curved wood panels which self-consciously evoke Konrad Wachsman and Walter Gropius for a writer's loft in New York's West Village. And because the client asked for 100 linear feet of shelving, he developed a shelving system made of custom aluminium extrusions. It was a great success. 'Ellen's brackets' are now in production, and the writer Ellen Levy is now his business partner.

A side chair, which Tayar notes 'has to respond to the body' (though, as we all know, a lot of architect-designed chairs do not) employs an idea from curtain wall technology. But the clever idea of using the same form (a thin slab that turns down at the ends) for both parts of the seat and the back rest had to be abandoned when ICF asked him to make the chair stackable.

Designing small objects, such as an ashtray that flips over to become a candle holder, made Tayar realise how the relationship between hand tooling and manufacturing was changing: 'Ten years ago, models for mass-production were made by hand. Now craft is being replaced by software, and that will allow for customisation.' He wonders how we will customise furniture. Chairs in size '38 Long?'.

The Parallel Design Partnership has designed lamps, storage systems, plywood tubing, restaurants (Waterloo, Midway, and PoP), and offices. A perforated ceiling which incorporated PoP's lighting, air-conditioning, and sound systems was transformed into an office system for a dot.com using the same computer technology.

Tayar's group recently completed a shelter for a residential courtyard in downtown Denver and is now working on an actual building – a house on Block Island with bold cantilevered structures that form a porch, a balcony, and a bridge to a guest cottage, while harnessing the two structures together. Δ

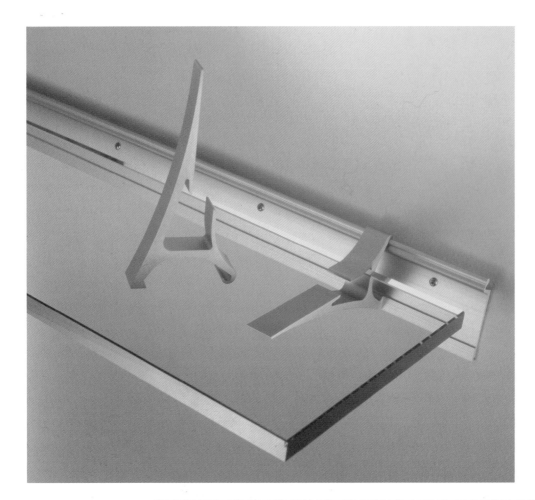

Top
Ellen's Brackets 1994. This
wall-mounted shelving system
consists of tracks and brackets
made of extruded and milled
anodised aluminium. The
shape of the bracket is based
on force-flow diagrams. When
the brackets went into
production, the design was
modified because the
manufacturer wanted an
adjustable system. The mass
-produced wall-mounted
horizontal system combines an
aluminium railing with a
simplified injection bracket that
can be used to create a single
cantilevered shelf surface.

Bottom
Michael's Table 1991. Inspired
by the cross-vault, the base of
this table is composed of four
moulded plywood shells
connected by CNC-milled
aluminium brackets. The
brackets then taper downward.
Though it isn't as easy to
flatten a cut-out as it is to
bend a cast piece, Tayar
created a folded plane at the
bottom so that the feet really
stand on the ground. Another
subtle detail separates the
vaults slightly from the table
top so that it doesn't seem
plunked. The table comes in
coffee and dining sizes.

Top left and right
Kinetic Records 2001. This alternative office system, called the Icon work/wall, was developed in 2000 for a research project on the 'low -rent-style' dot.com interiors. The president of a hip London -based DJ record label, Steve Lau, saw it in the Museum of Modern Art's 'Workspheres' show and commissioned Parallel Design to do the company's whole office – just before Kinetic Records was acquired by DMG/Bertelsman. Sheet laser-cut metal boxes are stacked up to create partition walls which double as vertical storage space and 'manage the mess'. A plywood desk surface spans the space between the wall and the filing cabinet to which it is fastened. The partition becomes structurally stable through the organisation of the desks like outriggers along its length.

Bottom
Gansevoort Gallery Gate 1996. This industrial-looking but mysterious gate provides security and a visual identity for a mid-20th-century furniture gallery in the edgy Meatpacking District of New York, where Parallel Design has its offices. Made of a sheet of perforated aluminium extrusions (a material typically used in industrial catwalks), the gate is suspended from a rust-coloured, 800-pound counterweight which is connected to a lever crossing the building's facade. In its down position, the teasingly translucent gate protects the gallery's display window and entrance; pushed up (with the touch of a hand), it creates an eyebrow over the now -transparent facade.

For more information on Ali Tayar go to *www.alitayar.com*

Architects and Furniture:

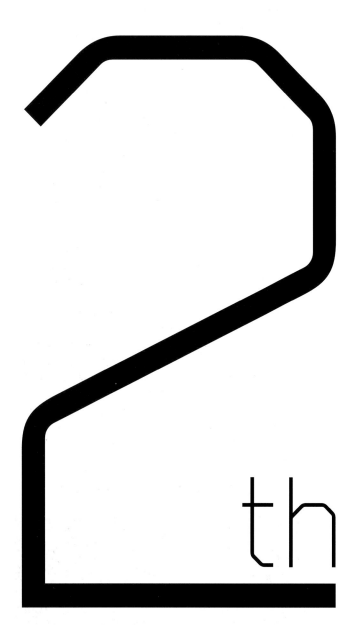

th

The historian **Alan Powers** lifts the veil on the modern masters by examining the mechanics behind the production and retail of furniture design.

He demonstrates just how crucial the part of an energetic entrepreneur or the right manufacturer was for transforming a modern design success into cult and then classic status.

a 20th-Century Story

There is a persistent tendency to simplify the story of design, in furniture no less than in other areas. 'Classic' status, once awarded, becomes self-reinforcing through museums, sale rooms and licensed reproduction and tends to be reflected back through historical accounts, which usually omit details of production beyond the original launch.

These pieces have become irretrievably implicated in a complex game of prestige and positioning and their later history will one day be recognised as an important aspect of the history of taste.

These pieces have become irretrievably implicated in a complex game of prestige and positioning and their later history will one day be recognised as an important aspect of the history of taste. They may be more durable than the tulips that were traded in 17th-century Holland, but their symbolic value is similarly divorced from their use value, and for this reason it is not in everyone's interest to lift the veil on the ways in which these few survivors came out on top of the evolutionary pile. Association with a famous architect or designer has certainly helped to forward the cult of the modern classic, despite being at odds with so many expressed Modernist intentions of anonymity and widespread availability.

What are the mechanics of the process by which architects have designed furniture during the 20th century? One might initially posit three different situations. First, architects design furniture in order to furnish their own buildings. This would cover most of the production of Charles Rennie Mackintosh and Frank Lloyd Wright, whose work was not available in the open market in their lifetime. Had Giuseppe Terragni's tubular steel chair for the Casa del Fascio in Como of 1930 been made commercially available at the time, his name would surely rank as a furniture designer on the strength of a single piece that was more visually and constructionally beguiling than its better-known contemporaries.

This category extends also to a number of other designs which began as being specific to individual buildings, such as Mies van der Rohe's Barcelona chair or Alvar Aalto's Paimio chair, both being put into production after their first appearance in the buildings (the Barcelona Pavilion 1929 and the Paimio Sanatorium 1931) after which they are named. Eileen Gray's designs were originally made in ones and twos for specific commissions, but only became more widely available after her death in 1976.

Second, architects design furniture speculatively at times of inactivity. Into this category would fall most of the furniture of Ernö Goldfinger, designed in London in the 1930s in the hope of making both money and reputation. After the Second World War, he became committed full-time to architecture, although still greatly interested in the details of furniture and fittings from an aesthetic and ergonomic viewpoint. Goldfinger's plywood pieces have in fact been manufactured from the late 1990s onwards by his grandson Nicholas. Peter and Alison Smithson seem to have designed furniture to fill the gaps between buildings, as well as developing a fine sense of its intrinsic value in their own work and that of the Modernist pioneers. In a later generation, Ron Arad studied architecture at the Architectural Association (AA) in London but on leaving in 1979 found that his predilection for furniture coincided with an absence of attractive architectural opportunities.

Third, furniture is designed in collaboration with a manufacturer and distributor with the primary intention of achieving retail or contract sales. The architects will no doubt specify their own pieces for their own buildings, but their activity is not distinguishable from that of a designer who is not an architect. In this category comes the furniture of Le Corbusier, Marcel Breuer, most of that of Alvar Aalto, and Charles and Ray Eames, as well as less well-known designers such as Josef Franck, Finn Juhl and Kaare Klint.

Opposite
Jack Pritchard, the founder of the Isokon Furniture Co at his home in Blythborough.

Right
Jack Pritchard's penthouse flat at Lawn Road Flats, designed by Wells Coates.

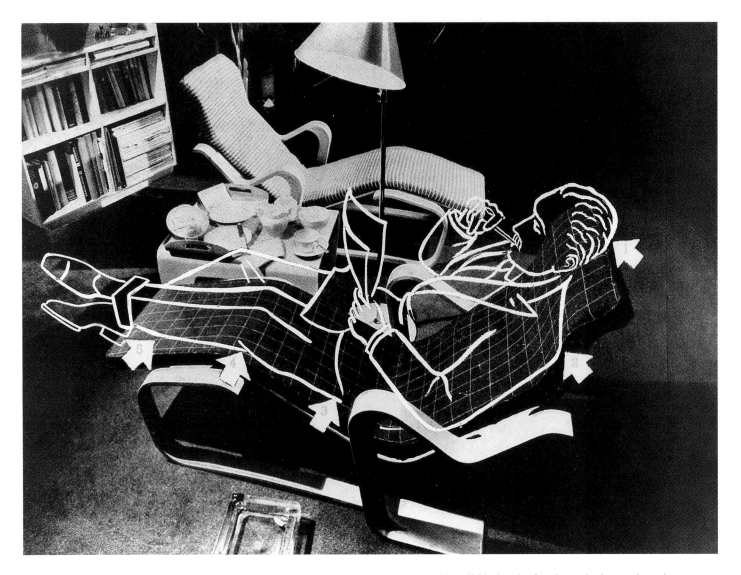

Not all Modernist furniture designers have been architects, and some have become architects only after beginning their careers with furniture and interiors. Robin Day, for example, has designed systems for specific buildings including the Royal Festival Hall (1951), and Gatwick Airport by Yorke Rosenberg and Mardall in 1957. Three outstanding contributors to the culture of architecture – Gerrit Rietveld, Pierre Chareau (co-designer of the Maison de Verre, Paris) and Jean Prouvé – were not architects, but brought to the conception of buildings a new set of ideas and priorities derived from a designer's way of thinking laterally about materials and realising their expressive qualities.

Prouvé said: 'there is no basic difference between the building of furniture and the building of a house'.

It was a Modernist article of belief that the conventional trade education in any field would probably only produce stale thinking, and that a designer with the right outlook could aspire to a set of skills which, because they were not too specific, might open up new forms and production methods. Chareau, Prouvé and Eileen Gray were consequently excluded for many years from the history of architecture.

In English Modernism of the 1930s, Wells Coates and Serge Chermayeff both designed furniture and interiors before launching into architecture, for which neither had any formal training. Chermayeff, having recently left Waring and Gillow, signalled his conversion to Modernist principles by setting up a company, PLAN Ltd,

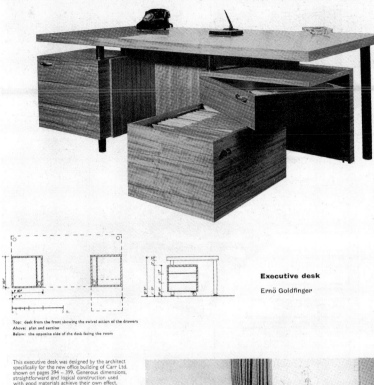

Executive desk
Ernö Goldfinger

Top: desk from the front showing the swivel action of the drawers
Above: plan and section
Below: the opposite side of the desk facing the room

This executive desk was designed by the architect specifically for the new office building of Carr Ltd. shown on pages 394 – 399. Generous dimensions, straightforward and logical construction used with good materials achieve their own effect. Legs are aluminium tubing covered with Doverite and all the woodwork is Australian walnut veneered. The drawers open by swivel action, the lower drawer being designed to contain files. The locks in the top drawers serve to secure all the drawers.

92

in 1932 that manufactured under licence unit furniture designed by Franz Schuster of Vienna, a collaborator of Ernst May in the Frankfurt housing schemes, and chairs based on designs by Knoll of Stuttgart.

There have been other furniture designers who simply avoided getting involved in the architectural process at any point. In England, the most notable from the inter-war period was Gerald Summers, whose bent ply armchair of 1934 formed from a single piece sheet of material has belatedly achieved some of the fame accorded to Aalto and Breuer.

The involvement of an entrepreneur could make all the difference between a piece becoming famous only as a prototype, thereby frustrating the intention of multiple production implied in Modernism, and its actual multiplication. Furniture production attracted some part-time enthusiasts in the 1930s such as the historian Sigfried Giedion, with his Wohnbedarf company in Switzerland, who was able to use his contacts among architect members of the Congrès Internationaux d'Architecture Moderne (CIAM), of which he was founder and secretary. For Jack Pritchard, whose Isokon company was patron and manufacturer of Breuer's wooden pieces of the 1930s, this was one component in a varied intellectual and business life. Pritchard nurtured the production of the Breuer pieces through the remainder of his long life, and his descendants have once more arranged for their production in London. Neither of these men was a conventional businessman, and perhaps had they been more focused on profits they would not have chosen the furniture designs they did.

Among the post-war production stories, the Hille company is notable since it existed from the early years of the century onwards and made reproduction pieces, but in the hands of its third generation it changed over to modern design and a contract system of distribution after the Second World War. Robin Day became its chief designer, but only because Leslie and Rosamind Julius, young directors of Hille, saw his work at MOMA in New York in 1949.

The Thonet company was crucial to the wide distribution of a number of pieces which through this attention became 'classics', including Marcel Breuer's Wassily chair, No B3 (1925), and Mies van der Rohe's cantilevered chair No MR533 (1927). The Breuer chair was first made by Standard Möbel before Thonet took it over, and Alexander von Vegesack notes in his 1996 history of Thonet that it failed to sell widely until it was relaunched in the 1960s by Gavina of Bologna, with the name Wassily attached to it for the first time. Le Corbusier, a devotee of Thonet's bentwood café chairs, such as Model No14 (1859–60) and the Vienna Chair, Model No 9 (1902–03), with continuous back and arms, was involved from 1930 with Thonet for the production of seven of the pieces designed by Charlotte Perriand, Pierre Jeanneret and himself, and shown at the Salon d'Automne in 1929. The fact that the French company Thonet Frères had branches in many different countries through the multinational Thonet-Mundus, based in Vienna, was an added incentive to working with them, although George H Marcus, in his book *Inside Le Corbusier: the Machine for Living In* (2000) records that Mart Stam's much less well-known tubular pieces sold better from the Thonet catalogues during the 1930s. Piracy of the designs was also a problem from the beginning.

The later history of the pieces shows how in Le Corbusier's lifetime they shifted position from being modern to becoming 'modern classics'. Initially Corbusier's fan Heidi Weber in Zurich arranged a limited edition re-release in 1959, in collaboration with Hans Girsberger, the publisher of Le Corbusier's *Oeuvre Complète*. Charlotte Perriand's name was dropped from the attribution, although she continued to receive a third share of the royalties. Then in 1965, the year of the architect's death, Cassina of Milan, which has changed the course of furniture history by a series of such resurrectionist moves, began production with construction details modified by the master.

The production of Alvar Aalto's furniture offers one of

Herman Miller Collection

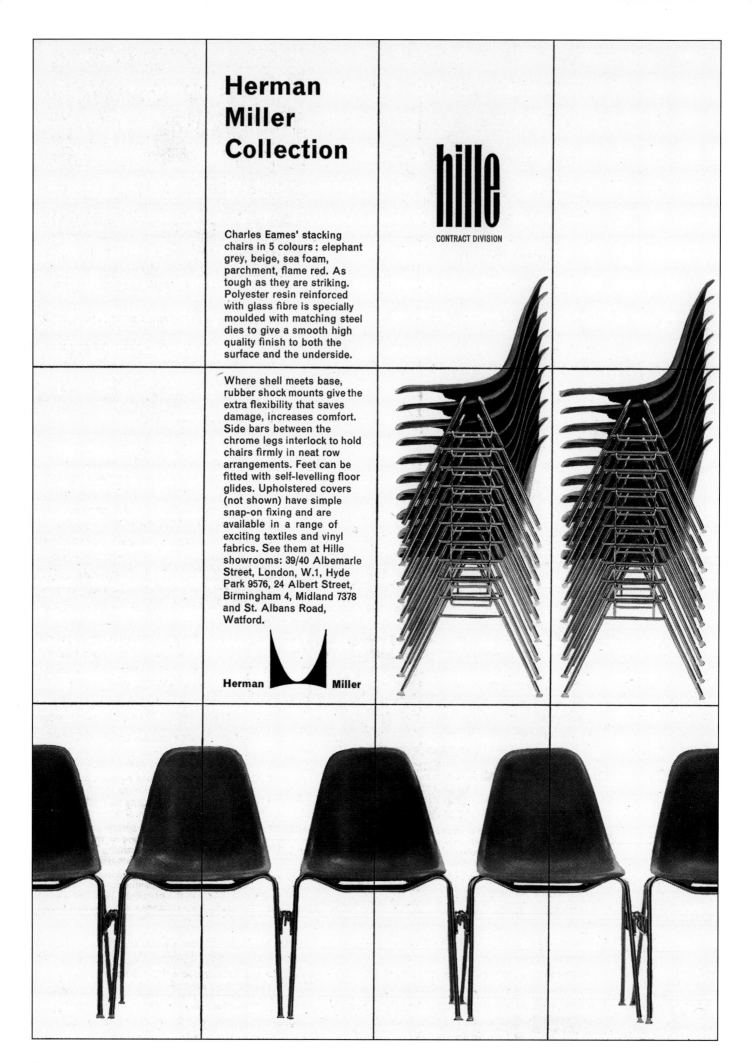

hille

CONTRACT DIVISION

Charles Eames' stacking chairs in 5 colours : elephant grey, beige, sea foam, parchment, flame red. As tough as they are striking. Polyester resin reinforced with glass fibre is specially moulded with matching steel dies to give a smooth high quality finish to both the surface and the underside.

Where shell meets base, rubber shock mounts give the extra flexibility that saves damage, increases comfort. Side bars between the chrome legs interlock to hold chairs firmly in neat row arrangements. Feet can be fitted with self-levelling floor glides. Upholstered covers (not shown) have simple snap-on fixing and are available in a range of exciting textiles and vinyl fabrics. See them at Hille showrooms: 39/40 Albemarle Street, London, W.1, Hyde Park 9576, 24 Albert Street, Birmingham 4, Midland 7378 and St. Albans Road, Watford.

Herman Miller

Opposite
Advertisement for Hille, featuring Charles Eames's stacking chairs in five colours (ad is black and white) for Herman Miller of America, *Architectural Design*, August 1962.

Right
Advertisement for Hille, featuring Charles Eames's chairs for Herman Miller of America, *Architectural Design*, March 1962.

Bibliography

Curtis, William, *Le Corbusier: Ideas and Forms*, Phaidon Press (London), 1986.

Davies, Kevin, 'Scandinavian furniture in Britain: Finmar and the UK market, 1949–1952', *Journal of Design History*, X, No 1, 1997, pp 39–52.

Davies, Kevin, 'Finmar and the Furniture of the Future: the sale of Alvar Aalto's plywood furniture in the UK, 1934–1939', *Journal of Design History*, XI, No 2, 1998, pp 145–55.

Deese, Martha, 'Gerald Summers and makers of simple furniture', *Journal of Design History*, V, No 3, 1992, pp 183–206.

Lyall, Sutherland, *Hille: 75 Years of British Furniture*, Elron Press Ltd in association with the Victoria and Albert Museum (London), 1981.

Marcus, George H, *Inside Le Corbusier: the Machine for Living*, Monacelli Press (New York), 2000.

Powers, Alan, *Serge Chermayeff, Designer, Architect, Teacher*, RIBA Publications (London), 2001.

Schildt, Göran, *Alvar Aalto: The Decisive Years*, Rizzoli (New York), 1986.

Smithson, Peter and Unglaub, Karl, *Flying Furniture*, Walter Köning (Cologne), 1999.

Sudjic, Deyan, *Ron Arad, Restless Furniture*, Fourth Estate Ltd (London), 1989.

Van Geest, Jan, *Jean Prouvé, Möbel/Furniture/Meubles*, Taschen (Cologne), 1991.

Von Vegesack, Alexander, *Thonet: Classic Furniture in Bent Wood and TubularSteel*, Hazar (London), 1996.

Weston, Richard, *Alvar Aalto*, Phaidon Press (London), 1995.

the most consistent stories of close collaboration and continuity. His earliest designs were a deliberate attempt to remedy what he saw as the coldness of tubular steel furniture (several pieces of which he owned himself) by using wood, ironically going back to the material the use of which by Thonet inspired the metal chairs. The stacking chair was commissioned by Otto Korhoren, the technical manager of Huonekalutehdas in Turku in 1928, and first used in one of Aalto's buildings in the Turku exhibition of 1929. The sequence resumed in 1931 with the pieces for Paimio, and in 1933 Aalto's pieces began to be exhibited and sold internationally, including a showing at Fortnum and Mason in London which led to the establishment of the Finmar company in England, partly under the direction of the architectural writer P Morton Shand.

Research by Kevin Davies has revealed that Finmar supplied 24 retail outlets, in London, Bristol and Edinburgh. Aalto's pieces were remarkably cheap, partly owing to the low labour costs in Finland at the time, but supplies were erratic until Shand and his associate Geoffrey Boumphrey suggested to the Helsinki gallery owner Maire Gullichsen that she should start the Artek company to manage production, which nonetheless remained based at Korhonen's factory as before. This turned out to be an inspired move, for not only has Artek served Aalto's reputation well by continuing production, but the introduction provided the basis for the Gullichsen's commission of the Villa Mairea. Finmar was restarted in London in 1949 by the Dane, Paul Ernst Stemann, originally a journalist. Aalto's furniture was less favoured during the 1950s and 60s than Danish and Swedish pieces that suited the style of the period better.

In addition to Cassina, the TECTA company in Germany has enriched the range of design classics with pieces by Prouvé, Breuer, Mies (with Lilly Reich) and the Smithsons.

None of these stories of skilful interweaving between the designer and the consumer can compare, however, with the focus brought by the Vitra company to the whole concept of modern furniture, and particularly the modern chair, in the last two decades of the 20th century. The importance of the subject has been emphasised at Vitra by a combination of scholarship and production that has skilfully conferred many of the attributes of antique furniture on pieces which, in their contemporary production, have escaped the taint of being 'reproduction'. The combination of international touring exhibitions, servicing the design museums of the world, with 'collectible' buildings at the company's headquarters at Weil am Rhein by Frank Gehry, Zaha Hadid and Tadao Ando, has provided the requisite number of layers of cultural dressing for a series of designs that makes the whole enterprise more typical of Post-Modernism than of Modernism. The production of miniature versions of some of the company's favourite models by Bertoia or Eames exemplifies a deliberate separation of the image of the furniture from its function.

The history of pre-1939 modern furniture, particularly the pieces designed by architects, can now hardly be separated from its post-war meta-history, often leading to a wilful confusion between Modernism then and Modernism now, since pieces of fifty or more years ago are upheld as 'timeless' classics. The cult of the signature architect has contributed not a little to the canonisation.

Furniture has so frequently been seen as subsidiary to architecture that the counter-argument has never been fully tested. Richard Weston's monograph on Aalto (Phaidon 1995) shows how Aalto's important shift from Functionalism to organic form, inspired by Moholy-Nagy, first bore fruit in his furniture designs. Did Charlotte Perriand's choice of pony skin as a covering for the chaise longue in 1928 help to stimulate Le Corbusier in a similar direction, as William Curtis suggests? Peter Smithson may have the last word in his book *Flying Furniture* (1999) with Karl Unglaub, quoting from a text of 1965:

what I most admired about Rietveld was his quietness. His seemed to me to be the only pattern of behaviour for a true architect. Rietveld touched only small things, each was given a life of its own, enriching the town (usually his home town) for its own ordinary sake. But it sometimes turned out to be a world event touching everyone. ⌖

Interview with
Vittorio Radice
of Selfridges

Vittorio Radice, the managing director of Selfridges, almost single-handedly led a retail revolution in the 1990s. Realising design's potential as a magnet for customers, he transformed the Oxford Street store into a 'site of cultural as well as commercial consumerism'. Within this remit, modern furniture came to the foreground with a treatment not unlike that of designer clothing flagged by brand and design. Edwin Heathcote talked to Radice about his vision for Selfridges expanding in the 21st century with a large-scale project by Foster and Partners on the London site and new stores for Manchester and Birmingham.

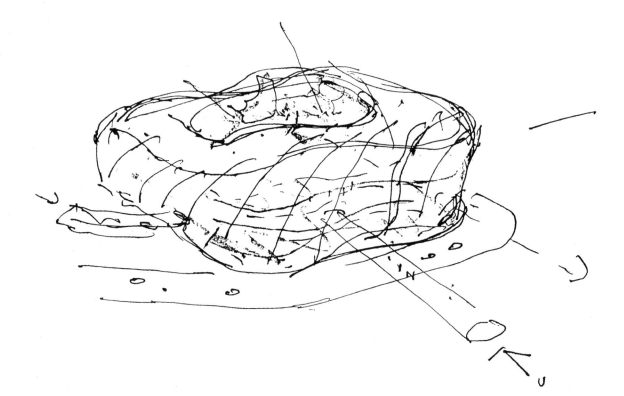

29 — 10 — 99

As shopping usurps the position of organised religion with all the attendant rituals and temples of consumerism, retail is becoming an increasingly important area for architects. Shops have become a remarkably important mode of architectural expression, arguably as important as the museum or art gallery (previous holder of the title of successor to the church as the zenith of an architect's career). Neil Cummings (who has written an essay on furniture and reuse for this volume) wrote a book with his partner, Marysia Lewandowska, *The Value of Things* (Birkhäuser (Basel), 2000) on the parallel development of the department store and the museum, using Selfridges and the British Museum to illustrate the two temples of consumerism (commercial and cultural). The managing director of Selfridges, Vittorio Radice, is revitalising the store through collaborations with artists and architects and cleverly making it a site of cultural as well as commercial consumerism, blurring the distinction between shopping and culture and between public and private urban space.

On the horizon for the rapidly expanding Selfridges brand is an entirely new store in the centre of Birmingham, designed by Future Systems, an incredible amorphous, ceramic disk-clad blob which will do much to define the rebuilt centre of Birmingham. A Manchester branch (situated in an existing building) also promises much through interior work by David Adjaye. Adjaye is already working on the London store which has also seen contributions from Ron Arad, and a new building behind Oxford Street designed by Norman Foster is currently under construction.

I asked Radice about the relationship between the department store, architecture and design.

'There have not been many department stores built recently, every new store opened in the last, say, twenty years, has been a part of a shopping centre, an adaptation of the design of the centre. But at the beginning of the century there are plenty of examples of department stores designed by wonderful architects. I recently gave a lecture in Birmingham on this subject and used the Carson Pirie Scott store in Chicago [designed by Louis Sullivan] as an example. Unfortunately that store has been neglected but it's wonderful; the architecture is as effective today as it was a hundred years ago. Unfortunately something needs to be done inside, it needs to be rejuvenated. This store [Selfridges] was designed in 1906, it was already a kind of Post-Modernist architecture then, a very impressive, well-scaled and proportioned building.

There have not been many department stores built recently, every new store opened in the last, say, twenty years, has been a part of a shopping centre, an adaptation of the design of the centre. But at the beginning of the century there are plenty of examples of department stores designed by wonderful architects.

'What we have to realise is that the architecture follows the time. It is about the associations people want to have. They associate themselves with the Tate Modern, with a museum, with a place, a hotel a particular restaurant or a label of clothing or a postal address. And it's the same with the store; you want people to be able to say I was there, there is an idea about creating a sense of place. You don't walk away wearing Selfridges because we don't make anything ourselves, Selfridges as a brand represents the place, and because it represents the place we cannot put ourselves in just any box when it becomes available. By bringing the brands together we create a sense of place; 80% of the people coming into Selfridges are on a day out, they're not out shopping. The fact that they shop is almost immaterial. We should bring them into the place out of curiosity, out of willingness to discover new experiences, new products, to meet friends. The architecture defines a role of containing this experience.'

I questioned Radice about the role of the store as public space in a world in which public space is being increasingly privatised.

'All department stores are an integral part of the fabric of the city. I always give the example of Isfahan in Iran. There is a beautiful square, the second largest square in the world after Tiananmen. The Shah built this square about four-hundred years ago when he wanted to move the capital of Persia there. In order to build the square he built his palace on the north of the square, the museum and school on another side, a mosque on the other and on the final side, the entrance to the grand bazaar, an old, intricate bazaar which was already there. And guess what, if you go to Red Square in Moscow you have the Kremlin, the historical museum, St Basil's Cathedral and the GUM department store. Commerce, the bazaar or the department store, this idea of exchange, of travel, this is the anchor of life in the city, the hub. And that's why it's very important to us when we move to Birmingham, to Glasgow or wherever, to talk to the council, because we are moving, if you want, the centre of the city, the traffic, the dynamic and the attitude towards the city centre.'

So you see the store as public space?

'It is public space, always public space. Department stores were founded on three principles. I was reading that when they opened Marks & Spencers stores they put up signs saying "free entrance". Because before, as soon as you went into these small shops you were asked "How can I serve you?". Why are you here, basically. It was intimidating. Private space.

'For us sightseeing is more important than shopping. Everybody is welcome. We know that 52% of people who enter will shop. So what is the job? To bring in as many people as possible. And because we know that 80% of people are there on a day out we need to design something that brings those people in. To surprise people, shock people, interest people, generate curiosity, that is our daily job because once they are here they will buy something.'

So how do you use architects to do that?

'Well for example, by using Future Systems, their way of seeing the world, we generate curiosity. Already people seeing the structure technology, to use it as a tool as we'd use a pen.'

Then I ask about another designer, David Adjaye, who was spotted by Radice.

'David Adjaye is incredible. He's doing three big projects for us. In Manchester he's doing the ground floor, the arrival area, a very important point. When we were talking earlier, we were talking about Carson Pirie Scott, wonderful outside but a non-event as soon as you pass the door. That's poor because the expectation created by this gigantic building is let down. It can't be just stuffed full of rolls of fabric like a supermarket. It shouldn't be so much a buying experience as a travelling, a visual, a dynamic experience. The ground floor of every department store is its business card.

'In Manchester there is an imposing building, but we are sharing it with Marks & Spencers and we need David to do a very difficult job, to create something on the ground floor which makes you say "Wow, I understand the difference between Selfridges and all other retailers". Then he's doing the second floor here in London, the *crème de la crème* of brands, the superbrands which are always on the front of *Vogue* and so on. We are creating a kind of internal square

It's about a new way of producing an environment which is about televisions and entertainment and technology, and making it much more familiar. After all, our houses are going to be full of technology soon, well they're already full, but it changes everyday. However, we need to be much more attached to that technology, to use it as a tool as we'd use a pen.

going up they're saying "What the hell is that?". When they see this amazing skin covering the structure they're going to think "Oh my God, what is that?". And when you finally open, people are just going to want to be there. In the same way their curiosity was stimulated by this store (Oxford Street) when it was built – it was surrounded by cottage-scale shops. It changed the scale of Oxford Street, eventually the rest of Oxford Street was forced to catch up – and that will happen in Birmingham too; it will stimulate its surroundings. There are still a few small houses and pubs but they will disappear, it's incredibly exciting.'

I ask about the new technology department, designed by furniture designer Ron Arad.

'It's about a new way of producing an environment which is about televisions and entertainment and technology, and making it much more familiar. After all, our houses are going to be full of technology soon, well they're already full, but it changes everyday. However, we need to be much more attached to that and then all around the perimeter are these interesting shops, it could be a fashion store, a bookshop, whatever.' (Adjaye is also working on a remodelling of Radice's own flat.)

I then moved on to furniture. Radice has brought in (and is still bringing in) a number of the best-known modern brands in furniture design and, remarkably, is making Selfridges one of London's prime places to go for modern design. I asked him about this new direction.

'It's been a long journey because we were a classic name, the building itself expressed classical design, we were seen as (and were) very traditional. So slowly, slowly we had to change not only the minds of people inside, that we could be a little braver and explore new avenues, but also bring the customers with us because, obviously, the last thing you want to do is to produce something different and the customers say "What the hell is that?". So we've been very careful in changing our image. We want the fourth floor to become a very contemporary home floor. Of course the journey between selling toilet mats and a modern chest of drawers is a long one. We'd like those floors to be

Capellini, Cartel, Driade, that type of environment, but we need to have the customers, and protect the volume. We're shrinking the classic spaces again and Capellini is opening a new area. We're hoping to reduce the pastiche element and we'll open a lighting department with SCP, but it's a long process. What we're very keen on is continuing this idea of developing place. It's very simple to execute, but very difficult to express. We have these big promotions which cost a lot of money but all contribute towards this notion of developing place.

'The transformation here has been very interesting, very hard work, but very interesting. All the other places I've worked have been about one view of the world; here you get a much bigger picture.'

Finally, I have to ask how London (perennially promoting itself as a new capital of design) and Milan (Radice's hometown and the actual capital of design) compare.

'For me Milan is a little bit too monotone. There's a very heavy influence from design, from furniture, fashion, architecture, it's everywhere and it's a little bit too much; there is no unexpected anymore. If today the fashion is to wear sunglasses, everyone will wear sunglasses. Here, you go to Camden Town, to Bond Street, to the Tate gallery, to Portobello, there is a tremendous reference. If there's a new restaurant in Milan everyone goes; here there are five new restaurants every week. London is a unique place; London, Tokyo, Paris, New York, they are the only places where you could support a store like this. In Milan you'd go bust in a few days.' ⊿⊃

Aero
347–349 Kings Road, London SW3 5ES
+44 207 351 0522
info@aeroliving.com
www.aeroliving.com
Open: Mon–Sat 10–6
Aero prides itself on being the shop in London to buy all the design classics. These include Hilton, Arne Jacobsen, Eero Saarinen, Eileen Gray and Charles and Ray Eames.

Aimé
32 Ledbury Road, London W11 2AB
+44 207 221 7070
Open: Mon–Sat 10.30–7
Stock includes video lounge chair by Christophe Pillet, table by Effets Personnels, lights by Day Glow, French furniture and accessories.

ARAM
110 Drury Lane, London WC2B 5SG
+44 207 557 7557
admin@aram.co.uk
www.aram.co.uk
Open: Mon–Sat 10–6, Thur 10–7, Sun 12–6
Established in 1964, the ARAM store shows over twenty different designs ranging from Bauhaus classics to the latest offerings from Milan, and specialises in modern high-quality furniture and lighting design. It features the work of established and new designers from Alvar Aalto and Harry Bertoia through to Ron Arad and Jasper Morrison to the latest graduates. Architect's furniture: Marcel Breuer, Stam, Arne Jacobsen, Bertoia, Eero Saarinen, Mies van der Rohe, Frank Lloyd Wright, Charles Mackintosh and Norman Foster.

Atomic Interiors
Plumptre Square, Nottingham NG1 1JF
+44 115 941 5577
simon@atomic-online.co.uk
www.atomic-online.com
Open: Mon–Sat 9.30–5.30
Atomic specialises in contemporary furniture and lighting with an emphasis on classic designs. Stock includes Eames, Le Corbusier, Mies van der Rohe, Nelsen, Marcel Breuer, Isamu Noguchi, Arne Jacobsen and Eero Saarinen. A classics catalogue is available on request.

Babylon Design Ltd
301 Fulham Road, London SW10 9QH
+44 207 376 7255
info@babylondesign.demon.co.uk
www.babylonlondon.com
Open: Mon–Sat 10–6, Sun 12–5
Specialising in pieces from the 18th century to the present, Babylon Design focuses on 1940–60 Danish furniture such as Finn Juhl, Arne Jacobsen, Hans Wegner and contemporary architects like Torsten Neeland and Michael Anastassiades.

back2myplace
5 Ivor House, Bridge Street, Cardiff CF10 2EE
+44 2920 400800
simon@b2mp.com
website under construction/in development
Open: Tue–Fri 10–6, Sat–Sun 11–5
back2myplace specialises in beautiful interior products by designers such as Charles and Ray Eames, Le Corbusier, Arne Jacobsen, Isamu Noguchi, Ludwig Mies van de Rohe, Verner Panton, Castiglioni and Ross Lovegrove. As well as its larger range of furniture by Zanotta, SCP, Fritz Hansen and twentytwentyone, it has a great range of homewares, lighting, glassware and ceramics.

Bd Barcelona
Majorca Street, 20091 Barcelona
+34 934 586 909
bd@bdbarcelona.com
www.bdbarcelona.com
Bd Barcelona is the creation of a number of architects and professionals in the design field, with the aim of producing and marketing furniture objects and accessories for decoration to a criteria totally independent of those habitually applied in the sector. Its objectives consist on the one hand to republish around the world a selection of historic designs by the greats of the past, such as Antoni Gaudí, Giuseppe Terragni, Charles Rennie Mackintosh, Josef Hoffmann, Adolf Loos and even the genial painter Salvador Dalí. On the other hand, the firm is engaged in the production of contemporary projects by designers such as Alvaro Siza, Ettore Sottsass, Óscar Tusquets or Javier Mariscal.

B&B Italia
250 Brompton Road, London SW3 2AS
+44 207 591 8111
New showroom in Singapore (May 2002)
B&B Italia and Space Singapore
Millenia Walk, Level 2, 9 Raffles Boulevard, Singapore
www.bebitalia.it
Open: Mon–Sat 10–6, Wed 10–7, Sun 12–5
B&B Italia has been a leading company in the field of contemporary furnishings since it was founded in 1966. B&B works with a number of international designers to create their thoroughly contemporary collections including Antonio Citterio, Mario Bellini and Paolo Piva. In additon to the core furniture collections there is also a capsule collection of accessories, linens, lighting and stunning kitchens by Arclinea.

Bishop
Kalîpçi Sok, No 152/9 Tesvikiye
80200 Istanbul, Turkey
+90 212 2968298/99
www.bishopstore.com
Bishop was founded in 1997 to introduce the rapidly growing design industry in Turkey. Bishop features furniture and accessories conceived by Michael Young, Arne Jacobsen, Kaare Klint, George Nelson, Marrianne Abelsson and Holger Strom.

Bowles and Linares
32 Hereford Road, London W2 5AJ
+44 207 229 9886
info@bowlesandlinares.co.uk
website under construction/in development
Open: Mon–Fri 11–5
Bowles and Linares, best known for the Espiga floorlamp and glassware, also designs interiors, architectural fittings, furniture, lighting and accessories as well as carrying stock in its London showroom. Furniture is architecturally detailed, lighting is sculptured and ambient, resonating the manufacturing processes and material base. Collection designs are manufactured to order in small batch production, as are special commissions. The borosilicate drinking and accessories glassware range OBHETOS challenges conventions in definitive forms and is available from stock/to commission. Lighting and glassware is also wholesaled.

Branson Coates
1 Honduras Street, London EC1Y 0TH
+44 207 336 1425
info@bransoncoates.com
www.bransoncoates.com
Open: Mon–Fri 10–5.30
Nigel Coates has worked with some of the best furniture manufacturers in the UK and has designed many pieces specifically for Branson Coates architecture projects such as Bargo in Glasgow and the Jigsaw shops with their energetic yet benignly coercive interiors. Their designs for furniture have become identified by their playful qualities; by the overlaying of the extraordinary and the commonplace.

Showroom BULO
The Vanilla & Sesame Building, 43 Curlew Street, Butlers Wharf, London SE1 2NN
+44 207 403 6993
Open: Mon–Fri 8.30–5.30
BULO (head office)
Industriezone Noord B6, B-2800 Mechelen, Belgium
+32 015 28 28 28
info@bulo.be, www.bulo.com
Bulo is one of the major design and office furniture manufacturers in Belgium. London was Bulo's first branch abroad. Its location very much hits the mark: the Vanilla & Sesame Wharf, in London's Docklands, right next to Terence Conran's shops and restaurants. Because the company truly believes that in producing ergonomic, innovating design solutions it is contributing to the art of design, its showrooms regularly serve as a platform for training and discussions about new ways of working.

Cantoni
Dallas Showroom (also Houston, Irvine and forthcoming showroom in Los Angeles)
4800 Alpha Road, Dallas, Texas 75244
+1 972 934 9191
info@cantoni.com
www.cantoni.com
Open Mon–Fri 10–7, Sat 10–6, Sun 1–5
Cantoni boasts ever-changing and evolving designs – like the world of design itself. It features a new signature line of furniture and accessories by design innovator Karim Rashid, who has been recognised and profiled most recently by *Time* as a leader in the profession.

Central
33–35 Little Clarendon Street, Oxford OX1 2HU
+44 1865 311 141
design@central-furniture.co.uk
www.central-furniture.co.uk
Open: Mon–Sat 9.30–6, Sun 11.30–5.30
Designers include: Mies van der Rohe, Arne Jacobsen, Le Corbusier, Eileen Gray and Ray Eames. Manufacturers: Vitra, Hiton Mylius, Teckno, SCP, Viaduct, Driade, Pallucoitalia, Alessi, Magis, Kartell, Herman Miller, Flos, Artemide, Foscarini, Philippe Starck, Michael Graves, Peter Maly and Ligne-Roset.

Centro Modern Furnishings LLC
4729 McPherson Avenue, St Louis
Missouri 63108
+1 314 454 0111
info@centro-inc.com
www.centro-inc.com
Open: Mon–Sat 10–6, Sun12–4 (additional hours by chance or appointment)
Centro is the exclusive St Louis retailer of B&B Italia, Zanotta, Baleri Italia, Wittmann, Cappellini, Driade, Montis, Herman Miller for the Home, Vitra, and more than a score of other furniture and lighting manufacturers. Whether as a designer, architect, collector or appreciator of fine design, you will find something appealing here and probably something not appealing. Centro recognises that design, like art, is subjective. The Eames' designs are available at Centro for purchasing, ogling, and trying out.

Chaplins of London Ltd
118/120 Brompton Road, London SW3 1JJ
+44 207 589 7897
477–507 Uxbridge Road, Middlesex HA5 4JS
+44 208 421 1779
17/18 Berners Street, London W1T 3LN
+44 207 323 6552
sales@chaplins.co.uk, www.chaplins.co.uk
Open: Mon–Sat 10–6
Chaplins represents large manufacturing names such as Cassina, Giorgetti, B&B Italia/ Maxalto, Kartell and Fritz Hansen with famous architect-designers behind these companies including Le Corbusier, Charles Rennie Mackintosh, Frank Lloyd Wright, Massimo Scolari, Leon Krier, Antonio Citterio, Ron Arad and Arne Jacobsen.

Designfenzider
93 Grand Street, SoHo, New York NY 10013
+1 212 343 8785
www.designfenzider.com
Designfenzider marries contemporary conceptual design with precise functionality. Drawing inspiration from classical influences and iconic forms, designer Ron Gilad deconstructs function in clean, glamorous shapes, creating utilitarian conversation pieces that elicit thought, emotion and pleasure at the beauty and humour of the objects.

Goldfinger Ltd
49 Combe Avenue, London SE3 7PZ
+ 44 7941 098 366
www.goldfinger.ltd.uk
Goldfinger manufactures the furniture designs of Ernö Goldfinger, the great Hungarian Modernist architect working in postwar Britain. (See Rebecca Milner, 'The Architect as Furniture Designer: Ernö Goldfinger', pp 7–13).

Illums Bolighus
Amagertorv 10, 1160 Copenhagen, Denmark
+45 33 14 19 41
Open: Mon–Thurs 10–6, Fri 10–7, Sat 10–5, Sunday (in the Summer)12–5
This department store in Copenhagen is like a magnet for tourists and others who are on the lookout for Danish design. Stocks include Georg Jensen and Alessi designed articles in addition to Italian Flos lamps designed by Philippe Starck and Castiglioni.

Inhouse Edinburgh
28 Howe Street, Edinburgh EH3 6TG
+44 131 225 2888
Inhouse Glasgow
24–26 Wilson Street, Glasgow G1 1SS
+44 141 552 5902
info@inhousenet.co.uk
www.inhousenet.co.uk
Open: Mon–Wed 9.30–6, Thurs 10–7, Fri 9.30–6, Sat 9.30–5.30
Stockists of contemporary furniture representing architects' designs from 1900 to the present day. These include Otto Wagner, Hoffman, Charles Mackintosh and Frank Lloyd Wright to Ettore Sottsass, Michael Graves and Norman Foster.

Isokon Plus
Turnham Green Terrace Mews, London W4 1QU
+44 208 994 0636
ply@isokonplus.com
www.isokonplus.com
Open: Tue–Sat 11–5
Isokon Plus has manufactured Marcel Breuer's plywood furniture since the 1930s. (See Alan Powers, 'Architects and Furniture: a 20th-Century Story', pp 84–89). It also carries pieces by Hein Stolle (coffee table) and Arne Jacobsen (Egg, Swan, Series 7, AJ Lights) and Alvar Aalto.

izé workshop ltd
Riverbank House, 1 Putney Bridge
London SW6 3JD
+44 207 384 3302/0705 007 1127
ed@ize.info, www.ize.info
Open: by appointment
izé was founded to bridge the realms of architecture, manufacturing, design and the useful and the ordinary. Working with architects to develop products for specific buildings, izé then aims to make these products available to the wider public. It manufactures and sells products by designers including Max Bill, 6a, Kenneth Grange, Sergison Bates, Alvaro Siza, Eduardo Souto de Moura, Wilhelm Wagenfeld, Walter Gropius, David Adjaye and Antoni Gaudi.

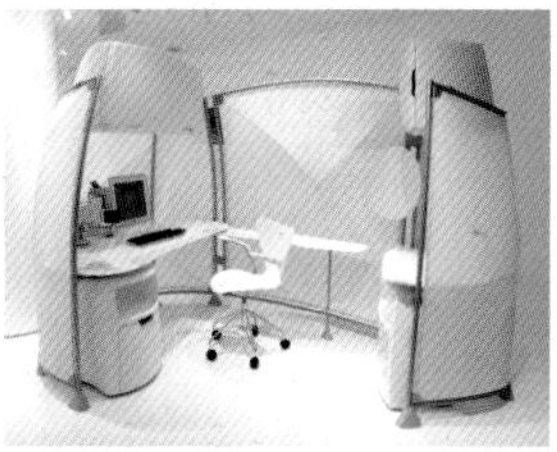

Knoll
A worldwide leader in the design and manufacture of office furnishings, Knoll offers elegantly conceived, creative products for office and residential use. Founded in 1938, Knoll's design philosophy is inseparable from its commitment to work with the world's pre-eminent designers. Designs with architectural designers represent Frank Gehry (Fog chair), Hani Rashid and Lise Anne Couture of Asymptote (A3 workstation, see illustration), Ludwig Mies van der Rohe (Barcelona chair), Eero Saarinen (Tulip chair), Gae Aulenti (Jumbo table) and Jonathon Crinion of Reff System.
enquiries@knolleurope.com, www.knoll.com
UK Knoll International UK Ltd/Knoll Inc
+44 207 236 6655
Belgium, Knoll International Benelux
+32 2 715 1300
Bermuda, Diversified Services (Bermuda) Ltd
+44 1295 9253
Croatia, OS Design Studio
+385 1 4826 443
Cyprus, El Greco Gallery Ltd
+357 231 4332
Czech Republic, Eternity
+420 2292 543
France, Knoll International France
+33 1 44 181999

Germany, Knoll International GmbH
+49 71 442 01243
New Zealand, Bromhead Design, Wellington
+64 4 384 7322
Bromhead Design, Auckland
+64 9 366 7322
Poland, Eweco Trading & Consulting
+48 22 625 3979

Kartell

Designers of international renown have
interpreted the Kartell style, with a
sense of timing and rhythm which has
succeeded in creating new products in line
with the company's core values of originality
in design and quality of materials. Of note is
Kartell's collaboration with internationally
famous designers such as: Ron Arad,
Antonio Citterio, Michele De Lucchi,
Ferruccio Laviani, Piero Lissoni, Vico
Magistretti, Enzo Mari, Alberto Meda,
Paolo Rizzatto and Philippe Starck. They
have developed original and innovative
ideas that have become familiar objects.
kartell@kartell.it, www.kartell.com
Denmark, Kartell Design Shop, Copenhagen
+45 33 931 931
Germany, Kartell Design Shop M. Roth,
Düsseldorf
+49 2118 6228500
Kartell Frank Ziegler, Frankfurt
+49 6921 977986
Kartell Lichthaus Moesch, Berlin
+49 3031 515120
Kartell at Punct Object, Hamburg
+49 40 3062 1260
France, Kartell, Paris
+33 1 4 5486837
Kartell Isotta, Perpignan
+33 4 68351120
Italy, Kartell, Milan
+39 02 6597916
Kartell Mobilberg, Bergamo
+35 215115
USA, Kartell, New York
+1 212 966 6665
Kartell/Retromodern.com, Atlanta
+1 404 724 0093
Kartell/Diva, Los Angeles
+1 310 271 0178
Kartell, The Design District, Miami
+1 305 573 4010
Japan, Kartell, Shinjuku Park Tower Ozone,
Tokyo
+81 3 5322 6808
Kartell, Kobe City
+81 78 845 2239
Kartell, Osaka City
+81 6 4391 9350
Taiwan, Kartell, Taipei
+886 2 87737559
Singapore, Kartell at Life Storey, Singapore
+65 732 7362

Lloyd Davies

14 John Dalton Street, Manchester M2 6JR
+44 161 832 3700
shop@llyoddavies.co.uk
www.lloyddavies.co.uk
Open: Mon–Sat 10–6 (Thur–7), Sun 12–5
Specialising in modern contemporary furniture,
Lloyd Davies stocks Mies van der Rohe, Arne
Jacobsen, Eero Saarinen, Le Corbusier, Frank
Lloyd Wright, Antonio Citterio and Paolo Piva
designs.

Luminaire

301 West Superior, Chicago, IL 60610
+1 312 664 9582
www.luminaire.com
Founded 25 years ago, Luminaire believes
that the more you learn about design and
its history, the more you will appreciate the
art of living and the importance of creating
beautiful environments. Its three showrooms
in Chicago, Coral Gables and Miami feature
the designs of internationally famous
designers such as Le Corbusier, Charles
and Ray Eames, Antonio Citterio, Piero
Lissoni, Eileen Gray, Paolo Piva, Ron Arad,
Achille Castiglione and Philippe Starck.

Mission

45 Hereford Road, London W2 5AH
+44 207 792 4633
www.infomission.com
Open: contact stockist directly
Mission blurs the boundaries of showspace,
shop lounge bar, architecture/design studio
and design PR agency. It sells a discerning
selection of old, new and rare books
about design and popular culture as well
as furniture, lighting and objects that are
timeless and elegant. Particular favourites
are the less familiar pieces of architect-
designed furniture by Knoll – Franco Albini
and Warren Platner.

Mooch

321 Bradford Street, Birmingham B5 6ET
+44 121 622 0390
info@mooch.eu.com
www.livingliving.co.uk
Open: Mon–Sat 10–6, Thurs 12–8
Mooch has an extensive range of classic
furniture by well-known architects Mies
van der Rohe and Le Corbusier. It also carries
contemporary items of furniture by Norman
Foster. Less familiar pieces of architect-
designed furniture are also available by
architects Enzo Berti and Piero Lissoni.

Places and Spaces

30 Old Town, London SW4 0LB
+44 207 498 0998
contact@placesandspaces.com
www.placesandspaces.com
Open: Tue–Sat 10.30–6, Sun 12–4
Specialists in sourcing original pieces from
the 20th century from Scandinavia, Italy and
America. Places and Spaces also supplies
re-issues and contemporary designs through
manufacturers such as Zanotta, Flos, Vitra
and Artifort.

Planet Bazaar

149 Drummond Street, London NW1 2PB
+44 207 387 8326
info@planetbazaar.co.uk
www.planetbazaar.co.uk
Open: Mon–Sat 11.30–7 or by appointment
Stocking 20th-century design classics by
designers such as Mies van der Rohe, Arne
Jacobsen, Eero Saarinen and Charles and
Ray Eames, Planet Bazaar also carries
plastic furniture by Verner Panton, Peter Ghyc
and Giotto Stoppino.

Pop UK

278 Upper Richmond Road, London SW15 6TQ
+44 208 946 1122
sales@popuk.com
www.popuk.com
Open: Mon–Sat 10–6, Sun 12–5
Contemporary and classic furniture from Isamu
Noguchi to Philippe Starck. Pop UK is an agent
for Vitra, Kartell, Flos, Foscanini, Montis,
Artifort, Driade, Pallucco, Artemide, Fasem,
Hitch Mylius and Alessi among many others.

Prego

Arch 17 Victoria Quays, Sheffield S2 5SY
+44 114 275 5512
pregohome@aol.com
Open: Tue–Sat 10–6, Sat 10–5, Sun 11–4
Specialising in modern domestic furniture,
Prego stocks items by Le Corbusier, Mies van
der Rohe, Eero Saarinen and Charles and
Ray Eames, as well as by contemporary
architects David Chipperfield, John Pawson,
Antonio Citterio and Gunilla Allard.

R 20th Century

82 Franklin Street, New York, NY10013
+1 212 343 7979
R 20th Century specialises in an international
selection of unique and well-crafted objects,
lighting and furniture from the mid-century
Modern movement. Its extensive inventory
of magnificent icons of this era includes
architect-designers Mies van der Rohe,
Arne Jacobsen, Eero Saarinen, Charles and
Ray Eames, Verner Panton, Marcel Breuer,
Frank Gehry, Eileen Gray, Isamu Noguchi,
Mario Bellini and Hans Wegner.

Schiang

58 Holywell Hill, St Albans, Herts AL1 1BX
+44 8702 202055
info@schiang.com
www.danish-design.com
www.swedish-design.com
Open: Wed–Sat 9.30–5.30, Sun 11–4
Schiang specialises in Scandinavian furniture.
It is the retail store for Cale Associates, the
largest UK importer of items by Danish designer
Hans J Wegner and Swedish designer Bruno
Mathsson. In addition, Schiang represents Niels
Moller and Jorgen Gammelgaard of Denmark.

Shannon

68 Walcot Street, Bath BA1 5BD
+44 1225 424222
sue@shannonuk.com
www.shannonuk.com
Open: Mon–Sat 10–5.30, Mar/Dec Sun 11–5
Shannon specialises in modern Scandinavian
classic furniture and lighting. Furniture
includes that by Hans Wegner, Bruno
Mathsson, Arne Jacobsen, Alvar Aalto, Erik
Magnussen, Eero Saarinen and Peit Hein.

Skandium Ltd

72 Wigmore Street, London W1U 2SE
+44 207 487 4646
skandium@btinternet.com
www.skandium.com
Open: Mon–Sat 10–6.30, Sun 12–5
Skandium specialises in the classics of modern
Scandinavian design including furniture,
lighting, kitchenware, glassware, textiles, rugs
and other decorative items. As well as classic
objects from world-renowned designers,
including Alvar Aalto, Verner Panton, Poul
Henningsen and Arne Jacobsen, Skandium
carries products from a new generation of
Scandinavian stars, among them Gunilla
Allard, Thomas Sandell, Harri Koskinen,
Björn Dahlström, Ingegerd Råman, Pia Wallén
and the trio Claesson Koivisto Rune.

The Conran Shop

81 Fulham Road, London SW3 6RD
+44 207 589 7401
www.conran.com
Open: Mon–Tue and Fri 10–6
Wed–Thu 10–7, Sat 10–6.30, Sun 12–6
A substantial homeware and furniture store,
The Conran Shop focuses on the overall
quality of its modern goods rather than
the sale of architect-designed items. In its
furniture department can be found pieces
by Arne Jacobsen, Phillipe Starck, Jasper
Morrison and, of course, Terence Conran.

The Home

Salts Mill, Victoria Road, Saltaire,
Bradford BD18 3LB
+44 1274 530770
home@saltsmill.demon.co.uk
www.saltsmill.org
Open: Mon–Sun 10–6
Carrying leading 20th-century classics from
Garrit Rietveld and Charles Mackintosh to
Castiglioni and Maui, The Home gives particular
emphasis on Alvar Aalto and Arne Jacobsen.
It also stocks the best of the contemporary
designers – Memphis designer George Sowden,
originally from nearby Leeds – and a very
comprehensive range of pens and watches,
all designed by architects including Ettore
Sottsass, Richard Meier, Michael Graves,
Charles and Ray Eames and Frank Lloyd Wright.

Totem Tribeca

71 Franklin Street, New York 10013
+1 212 925 5506

Totem SoHo

83 Grand Street, New York 10013
+1 212 219 2446
www.totemdesign.com
Open: Mon–Sat 11–7, Sun 12–5
Totem, a multifaceted company dedicated to
promoting design through physical stores,
exhibitions and educational multi-media, was
founded in 1997 by David Shearer to explore
the meaning that inherently resides behind
the best design available to the market through
an educational process that focuses not just
on objects but on the people and processes
behind the design.

twentytwentyone

274 Upper Street, London N1 2UA
+44 207 288 1996
18c River Street, London EC1R 1XN
+44 207 837 1900
shop@twentytwentyone.com
www.twentytwentyone.com
Open: Mon–Sat 10–6
twentytwentyone stocks the full range of
20th- and 21st-century designers from Marcel
Breuer, Alvar Aalto, Mies van der Rohe through
to the mid-century masters such as the
Eameses right up to the present contemporary
designs by Lissoni and Barber Osgevy. It works
directly with designers to produce a growing
collection of furniture and product designs,
and offers a direct design service to both
the public and to architects and designers
catering for specific project requirements.

The Room Store

Grand Hall, Albert Dock, Liverpool L3 4AA
+44 151 708 0000
www.theroomstore.co.uk
Open: Mon–Sat 10–5.30, Sun 11–5
The Room Store is a comtemporary retailer of
furniture and homewares. In terms of classic
designed furniture, it stocks Le Corbusier's
chaise longue and Mies van der Rohe and Ray
and Charles Eames designed furniture.

Vitra

Founded in 1950, Swiss furniture manufacturer
Vitra has played a key role in the production of
architect-designed furniture and its promotion.
Having produced the furniture of Charles and
Ray Eames since the late 1950s, and Verner
Panton's chairs since the late 1960s, it is now
manufacturing pieces by a full cast of
international architects and designers
including Emilio Ambasz, Ron Arad, Mario
Bellini, Antonio Citterio, Frank Gehry, Norman
Foster, Jasper Morrison and Philippe Starck.
The relationship between architecture and
furniture does not end at furniture manufacture
itself. Since commissioning Nicholas Grimshaw
to produce a production hall at Weil am Rhein
in 1981, the company has been an active patron
of architects. Buildings at Weil am Rhein
include Frank Gehry's Vitra Design Museum
(1989) and a production hall, Zaha Hadid's
Vitra Fire Station (1993), Tadao Ando's Vitra
Conference Centre (1993) and a production hall
by Alvaro Siza (1994). Through the foundation
of design museums at Weil am Rhein and
Berlin, and its involvement in travelling
international exhibitions, Vitra has also been
instrumental in raising public awareness of
design and architecture.
www.vitra.com
Spain, Vitra Hispania SA, Madrid
+34 91 426 45 60
Vitra Hispania SA, Barcelona
+34 93 268 72 19
France, Vitra, Paris
+33 1 56 77 07 77
Germany, Vitra GmbH, Berlin
+49 30 29 36 91 0
fucon GmbH furniture concepts, Hannover
+49 511 39 089 550
Vitra GmbH Düsseldorf
+49 211 30 206 40
Switzerland, Vitra AG, Zürich
+41 1 277 77 00
UK, Vitra Ltd, London
+44 20 7608 6200
USA, Vitra Los Angeles
+1 310 652 7997
Vitra New York
+1 212 539 1900

Below
Peter Eisenman and Charles Jencks in
Eisenman's office in New York, Spring 2002.

The New Paradigm and September 11th: Peter Eisenman in conversation with Charles Jencks

Charles Jencks interviewed Peter Eisenman on issues on Deconstruction – in December 1987 and May 1989 – and these exchanges, like the following that took place in November 2001, are often cryptic. Like a Pinteresque conversation: more is implied than said.

CJ: Peter, under question is the new paradigm in architecture, your work and September 11th. You often put things in a historical context and argue that we've shifted – or ought to have shifted – from a mechanistic to an electronic paradigm.

PE: There are many shifts. Clearly, information and the way information is processed – ie through computers, through the Internet, through design techniques, computation – has changed the world quite a bit. This had a lot to do with September 11th. The fact that we saw the planes go into the World Trade Center at the same time as somebody in Japan or Los Angeles did means that we were all witnessing live a media event that was staged destruction. With Auschwitz and Hiroshima we saw the events later, in a film or in photos. In effect, media coverage of September 11th provided us with an instant memorial. We can never think about the World Trade Center without remembering those images of events as they were happening. That has rarely happened in the history of mankind.

CJ: So, you rather share the *Zeitgeist* argument that, for instance, photography forever changed the role of painting – one medium supplanting another is a historicist argument. We can't get rid of the images in our mind of the World Trade Center collapsing, and therefore that image is ingrained in our nervous systems for all time. It's not accessible to our imagination.

PE: 'Not accessible to the imagination' is not a historicist argument.

CJ: Well, you *are* arguing for a unique kind of occurrence. In a 1992 *Domus* article you wrote that the shift from a mechanistic to an electronic paradigm *should* be the shift. You use the word 'should'. In other of your writings you say that we're moving into an era of Folding Architecture – blurring or blending or intermixing – and you again use a normative phrase. Then you also say, as part of the shifts, we are in a new psychological state of destabilisation and that the role of architecture – or your architecture – *should be* to further destabilise. So all of those three things – electronic paradigms, folding and destabilisation – are part of what you see as the new paradigm?

PE: First of all, architecture has always destabilised. Architecture first means to have an idea about something – that is, to theorise something in space and time. Second, it means not just to formalise the idea but rather to have a position about it – that is, to put it in a critical context. Architecture has always done this. It has never been just a historicising agent, but also a problematising one. Architecture never solved problems; it opens problems to their own repressive tendencies. The kind of architecture that creates history has always been theorised, has always been critical, has always been problematising. Brunelleschi destabilised the Gothic, then Alberti destabilised Brunelleschi, Bramante destabilised Alberti and so on to Borromini, to Schinkel...

CJ: In the past, you have put forward a historicising position – that is to say that architecture is going in a certain direction and it *should be* doing this and *shouldn't* be doing that (something I would argue is part of the critical). You've put forward the idea that there's a new space conception, no longer Euclidean, and that we must destabilise the Euclidean position *now*, because it's now, not then.

PE: Yes, because the Euclidean position, at one time, destabilised architecture. That is equivalent to what Newtonian physics did in its time, what Darwinian biology did in its time.

CJ: Exactly; so there *is* a historicising, evolutionary narrative in your argument – exactly like Sigfried Giedion's, who also used space/time concepts. Not only do you sound like Giedion, but you even use the narrative of space/time to do so.

PE: The fact that we now have a condition of terrorist activity – non-state-supported destruction – means that we have to consider in our time how we problematise that situation through architecture. In other words, how do we ask questions in architecture that we did not have to ask before. How does architecture symbolise, mean, etc.? When I first read Jacques Derrida's *Of Grammatology*, about the notion of trace, my architecture began to understand something about what I had previously been doing in a different context. It could not have understood this before I read Derrida. He opened up ideas, as do the new biologies, new geometries. If this is historicism, so be it.

The critical and the new paradigm

CJ: I want to pursue the new paradigm, but instead of trying to define it now, let's talk about who you see as the major players in this shifting field?

PE: Somebody like Peter Zumthor, for instance, makes beautiful use of wood, but it is used in a way that does not problematise. It is just beautiful wood for its own sake. The people who matter to me are those who take space and time and manipulate them to problematise what I would consider the conditions of the present. Who are those people for me? Rem Koolhaas, Daniel Libeskind, probably Bernard Tschumi, Jacques Herzog, or Enric Miralles, when he was alive.

CJ: Where does Jacques Herzog problematise architecture?

PE: He is working with the relationship of the vertical surface to the section. He experiments with the question of scale, materiality and the way openings are made in the vertical surface. His vertical surfaces are intricate screening devices, and in that sense they problematise the vertical surface.

CJ: What about Coop Himmelblau or Zaha Hadid?

PE: We need another category for Gehry, Hadid, and Coop Himmelblau – contemporary expressionists – who give their overarching integrity to architectural

Below
Le Corbusier, Philips Pavilion, 1958. Charles Jencks's
illustration of Le Corbusier's pavilion demonstrating
how he understood the 'new paradigm'. The pavilion
uses a biomorphic stomach form – a body form in
plan – and curved hyperbolic parabola in elevation.

expression. Among the younger architects I would say Greg Lynn, Foreign Office Architects. I might have Toyo Ito in there.

CJ: **We've been discussing the critical rather than the new paradigm position. The new paradigm, to define it, comes out of a new world-view, a new science, a new cosmogenesis, a new concept of emergence and the idea of self-organising systems. The computer, media and electronic paradigm are merely a leading part of this larger picture. Let me exaggerate a difference with you to bring out the point. I would say that Le Corbusier, with the Philips Pavilion of 1958, is one of the first people not only to build in the new paradigm, but also to understand it. He developed the light**

and sound show (an example of the new media). He used a biomorphic stomach form, a body form in plan and curved hyperbolic parabola in elevation (so he understood an emergent grammar related to biology). And he adopted the cosmic iconography in his light and sound show, a key aspect of the new paradigm. All of this in one building – 1958 – though he did not use the computer. I want to ask you about Koolhaas and his position in this – between the critical and the new paradigm, if we can slip between them a bit. For instance, Rem has opened up a door for so many architects in Holland, who are labelled the SuperDutch, such as MVRDV, WEST 8, Ben van Berkel and others. I wondered what your view of their architecture is, because it looks to be at the information end of the architectural spectrum, rather than at the deformation end – yes?

PE: I do not have a view of the Rem School. You cannot imitate Rem, because his strength is not in the forms but in the critical nature of the way they are deployed in a particular context. It is not so much the space that Rem makes, it is the context in which he makes it. The others are without Rem's deep cynicism. What makes critical architecture is not so much cynicism as a genuine belief in the possibility of architecture to problematise culture. Without any deformation or transformation we only have information.

CJ: **What about Rem's work as architecture? You were critical of it as avoiding the interiority of architecture. He may problematise aspects of the ground plane and urban landscape at the Kunsthalle or Jussieu...**

PE: Rem has never been interested in form per se, and how form informs or critiques. He is interested in how form can be used ironically or cynically. For example, *Delirious New York* is full of both. Many of his projects are stunning amalgams of irony, wit and spatial pyrotechnics – the Jussieu Library, the Karlsruhe Technical Centre, the Kunsthalle in Rotterdam. Rem has the capacity not to make architecture so much as a kind of critical distance from formal manifestations as iconic in themselves. In this sense we are very far apart. Yet Jussieu, his first La Villette project, are stunning. Some others, such as Lille and IIT, are rather banal. We are not all perfect. Rem has done enough to change the world. Now, the terrorist act of September 11th has brought an end to the age of irony.

CJ: **Well, I can't help but be ironic when I hear you say that. Maybe September 11th has made cheap irony and cynicism more objectionable, but they're still very much present. Roland Barthes said, 'Cynicism is a pre-condition of truth in a commercial society', and that is not going away, no matter how many September 11ths we get.**

PE: A cartoon in the *New Yorker* featured a book in the window of a bookstore alongside a sign that said '50% less irony'. Great cartoon!

Paternity for the blob

CJ: **I hear what you're saying. Let me go on to the blobmeisters. I talked to Greg Lynn and asked him, 'who are the blobmeisters?' and when was the phrase first used. He gave me a potted history – having to do with you, by the way.**
PE: Well, 'blobmeisters', I believe, comes from Herbert Muschamp. He used the terms 'blobmeister' and 'nerb-terrorists'. I do not have much to do with blobmeisters.
CJ: **Well, they came out of your office. You were the paterfamilias. The blob comes out of the fold, and the fold comes out of your looking at your crisis – one of your many crises – in the autumn of 1988. Then, according to Lynn, you were analysing 'what next?', and going into the Guardiola house and all those things you used to deconstruct assumptions. And then you realised you'd accidentally killed off Decon by having that show on it at MOMA.**
PE: I do not think the fold has anything to do with the blob.
CJ: **But it relates to the blob because the grammar folds continuously from floor to wall to ceiling. Whereas a blob is a more conceptual fold that has a more seamless continuity.**
PE: Let's say it is a continuous fold.
CJ: **OK, but the blob conceptualises a new non-Euclidean geometry, and it pragmatises it, because it puts it on a computer and uses vectors instead of axes. Greg Lynn's blob is an attack on Colin Rowe and the whole tradition of Euclidean geometry. The blob is the new schmoo, isn't it? And it came out of your office. You had four young Turks in your office: Greg Lynn, Jeff Kipnis, Mark Wigley and Sanford Kwinter. And, according to Lynn, at the end of 1988 the four young Turks fashioned out of your psychoanalytic crisis the blob. You together made the fold and then they made the blob. Except the problem with the blob is that it has no scale, orientation or scaling. It's without articulation. It has the same problem that Gropius's blob diagrams have, which is that it's kind of pre-architectural.**
PE: It's aformal.

Haptic affect

CJ: **But the blob and fold lead into your notion of haptic and affective architecture.**
PE: Haptic and affect have to do with the question of the arbitrary. In André Gide's *Lafcadio's Adventures*, the guy decides to kill somebody on the train because he wants to commit a perfect crime. He gets caught because he's the only one who could have committed the crime, so there's no such thing as the arbitrary here. By contrast, what I've tried to do is to undercut the question of intentionality, that is, the motivation that exists in the ground of architecture, or in the sign, or in the object. In all these cases, I have been working

with 'the becoming unmotivated' of these areas. To do that, I work with the haptic – arbitrary texts, diagrams – these kinds of things. For me they are all part of what you would call the new paradigm. How I employ them is very different than how Greg Lynn would, and it's what we do in the end, not what we say – what we say in our doing – that's critical.
CJ: **OK, but 'the becoming unmotivated of the sign', or the haptic or the diagram – all of those things are highly intentional, in fact almost autocratic.**
PE: I said *becoming* unmotivated. There is no possibility of totally arbitrary, or totally unmotivated. The choices that I make move towards less motivation.
CJ: **I want you to talk about the body – the logic of topological space and why the body relates to it.**
PE: When you go into the Wexner Center or the Aronoff Center, there is a different experience that the body has in space. It feels different, even though formally and functionally it is the same scale and use of space as other campus buildings. Wexner is cool, abstract, distant. It was from a different moment in time, the mid-1980s. Later, the Aronoff opens up those calculations to the possibility of affect, to haptic experience, to the possibility of being lost in space. The affective dimension of the space is more active in Aronoff than it is in Wexner. There are times when you do not know where you are in that building.
CJ: **So that interest *does* overlap with Gehry's work, the blobmeisters, a lot of the people who are doing folding and non-Euclidean architecture. It's part of the new paradigm. I'm not saying that it's all the same – but it has intentions similar to, say, Miralles.**
PE: No, I believe that Bilbao is a great building, but I do not think there is an overlap between Aronoff and Bilbao.
CJ: **But they're both affective in different ways, yes?**
PE: They are affective in different ways. Bilbao is gestural, Aronoff is notational. The entire spatial condition of Aronoff is about reading as an affective experience. It may look and feel similar to Gehry, but its conceptual apparatus, its intentionality, is entirely different.
CJ: **Some of your buildings I would say characterise the new paradigm, for other reasons, are projects like Rebstock and Max Reinhardt, which are key for opening up the idea of folding, and the project for the painter Immendorf which, like my work, makes use of the soliton wave. But focusing on some that have been built, the Columbus Convention Center is definitely one of the first buildings in the new paradigm. It develops a vermiform grammar that relates to highways and American infrastructure, yet at the same time manages to break down the huge size.**

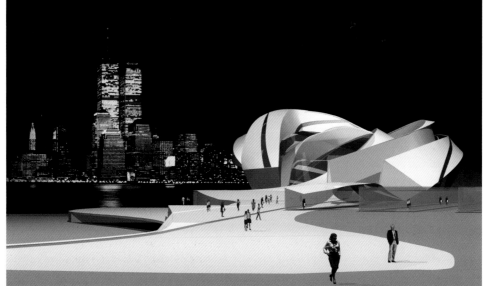

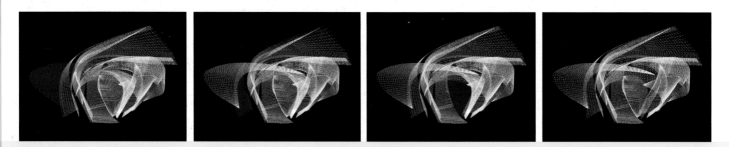

Below
Peter Eisenman, diagrams for Museum for Santiago de Compostela, Spain.
In addition to generative grids, it uses the Shell of St Jacques and the
medieval city plan.

PE: The Wexner, for instance, was critical because it cut between the existing buildings. It places something in the context that was not just new but changed the context entirely. Graves's project added to the context. We changed it. At the convention centre we attempted a similar thing. Instead of making an isolated object, we tried to make a building that attempted to modify the existing context. We did this in our Rebstock project, where we inserted something – a graft or a trace – that does not just add or subtract to the context but transforms it as a whole.

CJ: At the convention centre you use the vermiform grammar, just after Gehry's use of it in his Vitra Museum, and it has all the qualities you've mentioned. There's the trace and graft, but also, importantly, the semantic overtones that relate it to highways and fibre-optic cables and other things.

PE: The vermiform came out of a set of railroad tracks; they were the traces of railroad tracks that were on the site. The front end of that building was a railroad station that lined up on High Street and had these tracks criss-crossing behind it. I do not believe it had anything to do with Vitra conceptually.

CJ: But your later work, after 1989, is my kind of Post-Modernism – because it has semantic references or traces, which have a semiotic dimension. I know that some of your work explicitly distances itself from a semiotic position, but other buildings like the convention centre are clearly related to semantic meanings. This is of crucial importance and it distinguishes your work from so many of those following the computer paradigm: when you mix your semantic diagrams with your generative, syntactic diagrams the hybrid is much more interesting and challenging than a purely formal pursuit.

PE: I would say that my work is more grammatological than semiological. The writing of the buildings is neither representational nor iconic; it is indexical. The work differs from a semiotic, or narrative, intention.

CJ: Whatever your intentions, your indexical signs for the convention centre are another person's semantic readings: of 'railroad tracks', 'fibre-optics', 'highways and overpasses' and such like. I would insist that these semantic dimensions, an important part of the Post-Modern agenda, are what make your architecture more interesting than the syntax of blobs and folding. Every now and then your work has that semantic dimension, and it becomes a part of your diagramming – say in the Geneva Library project.

Your competition entry for the Rome church 2000 (which Meier won), disputes the role of the church in a positively semiotic way. What was your intention there?

PE: The idea was not to use the traditional signs of the church – a belltower or baptistry, say – but rather to take the church functions and weave them into a sacred space that was *not* iconic.

CJ: You actually split the community into two parts, which become the Christ and the Antichrist.

PE: There are two naves, yes. Early pilgrimage churches had split naves. The church was a very successful project, so successful, in fact, that the priest on the jury said, 'It doesn't look like a church, therefore it can't win'. But we won, because they recognised what we were doing.

CJ: I know there's more to it than we've discussed, but I want to look at the Staten Island project – the Arts and Sciences Center. First of all let me ask you what the status is on that. Is it getting built?

PE: Well, right now it's on hold, as are many other New York projects after September 11th. The money for the project had been appropriated. The question is whether the new administration will keep that money in the appropriation. Right now it is too early to tell.

CJ: For me it's one of your great projects, and as a piece of architecture I love the way it's been generated through different diagrams and deformations. It captures the movement of pedestrians, vehicles and all sorts of systems through the building. You say it's different from the Guggenheims of Frank Lloyd Wright and Frank Gehry because it doesn't have their kind of centroidal emphasis or atrium. It's fascinating that for you, as for Sigfried Giedion, space and space/time are still the primary narratives in architecture. This, as opposed to Venturi's interest in, say, the sign, or mine in meaning. You're still generating buildings as Giedion proposed, except the space/time concept has changed radically since the 1940s.

PE: Heisenberg and quantum mechanics are also involved with the theories of space / time.

CJ: Giedion and Bruno Zevi. What's so funny is that you sound like an old Modernist.

PE: If Heisenberg is out of date, then I am. They are

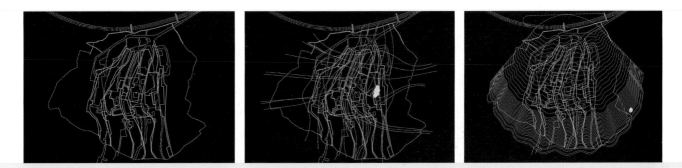

not, however, Giedion's space/time concepts. They are generative.

CJ: **So for Staten Island they seem to be a major player.**
PE: The difference between Staten Island and Wright's Guggenheim is important in this very sense.

Santiago and the Enigmatic Signifier
CJ: **Now, If we can turn to Santiago, again, it's a scheme of yours that I really enjoy in simulation. You won it in 1999 as a result of 'the Bilbao effect'.**
PE: Santiago wanted to produce a secular tourist attraction, other than the religious pilgrimage sites that bring in millions of tourists each year. Galicia saw how successful Bilbao was for the economy of the Pays Basque. We proposed an alternative to the figural object, a project that was a landscape – that was totally other than Bilbao.
CJ: **For me Santiago has extraordinary qualities. First it is a landform building, in the way that a lot of urban landscape buildings have been proposed by Rem and the SuperDutch, but secondly it's a literal landscape – because the ground comes over it. Thirdly, it has two semantic diagrams built into it. As well as the generative ones on deforming spacial grids, it uses the Coquille St Jaques – the Shell of St Jaques, which is the symbol of the city – and also the medieval city plan. So it folds those two diagrams into its other generative diagrams. Is that fair?**
PE: There is also a third ordering diagram, and that is the idea of the ley lines. The interiors of the project have developed from Druidic ley lines which led the people from France to Santiago. What we did was to extrapolate them. All of the deformations internal to the building are based on the deformations of these ley lines.
CJ: **Is that, and the other two diagrams, explicit? Or are they only operative from the air, or from your diagrams.**
PE: No. They are three-dimensional.
CJ: **Will people be given a map? Will they ever see a coquille shell or know it's the old plan of the city? Because communication works best oscillating between implicit and explicit signs. This creates the suggested sign, or enigmatic signifier, something that has become the new convention for public buildings since Ronchamp: the Sydney Opera House, Saarinen's TWA, Pelli's Blue Whale, or today the work of Gehry, Alsop and Coop Himmelblau. The enigmatic signifier typifies your work at Santiago. People will feel those suggestions. The affective answer is they will *feel* in the alleyways that they're in a kind of medieval situation in the present day?**
PE: They will feel in the alleyways something that is not quite medieval and not quite modern. It is something

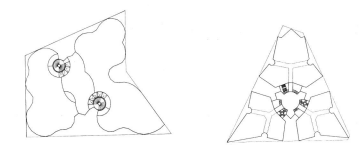

else. My idea of affect is that you experience something, you feel something, you see something but you cannot quite explain it. It has an Ur dimension to it. You know something other than function, structure, meaning, or beauty is present, but you cannot quite explain it.

Skyscrapers

CJ: **Two of your skyscraper projects take these ideas to the central city – one in Berlin, the other in New York. Both projects push the envelope of the tall building, as it were. You talk about the Berlin Tower in terms of 'the fluidity of today'. It is a clear mixture of two Mies schemes, a blur between them, that is then turned into the most fluid, elegant twist. I admire its deft creative simplicity, of smart interbreeding – and wonder if it's one of the clearest examples of blurring you've ever done.**

PE: Well, to have a *clear* example of blurring is an oxymoron. If it is clearly blurred it is probably not blurred enough. Both towers attempt a similar thing. Each takes two disparate plans and morphs them into one another with a simple morphing device. Depending on where you begin and how you work, the production is very different. This is very interesting, because it's not just a mechanical process. For Berlin we took the two Mies plans, and the section that was produced 50 per cent of the way between the two as end points of a morphing system. We took that section and then twisted or rotated it through its length to produce the final result. For the second one – the New York tower – we took the Queens' grid, which was already rotated, and the Manhattan grid, and rotated one off the other. We already had a twist in the object. Then we put compression on the top and the bottom, which accounts for its buckling form in the middle. Depending on how the initial point is treated – that is, how you choose to operate on these so-called diagrams, whether they are Mies grids or city grids – you can produce different results. A skyscraper usually has a base that is a lobby, a middle, and a party hat on the top. We were trying to put the energy in the middle instead of at the top and the bottom.

Philip Johnson made a very interesting comment about the Berlin tower. He said, 'You know, Mies would never have ended it rotated – you have got to bring it down orthogonally to the ground'. We changed the base because of his criticism. There is a subtle noticeable difference between the two towers. Both towers have maximum energy in the middle, but they are not twisted; there is rotation in the Berlin Tower and there is compression in the East Side Tower.

CJ: **And this emphasis on the middle is certainly different from all other skyscrapers, which emphasise**

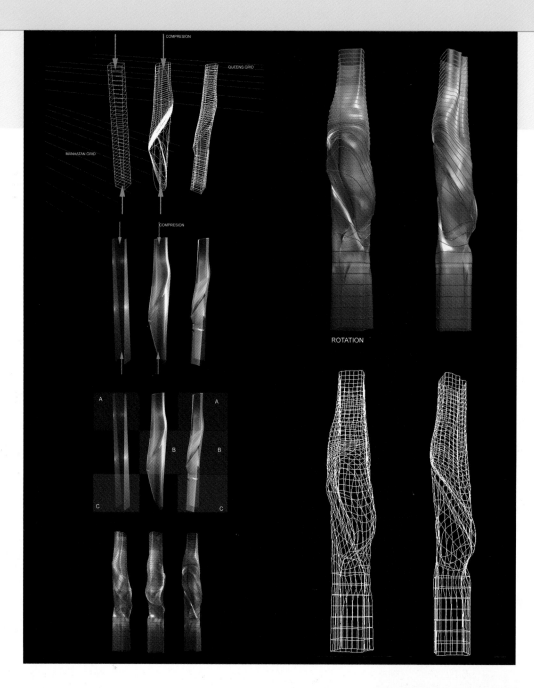

the bottom and the top. It goes with your idea that, in a way, everything is all middle.

PE: None of our projects have what you could call endings or beginnings; they are all middles.

CJ: You dislike what Frank Kermode called in a book of that name, 'the sense of an ending', the drama of something coming to closure. You've recently – in the last ten years, that is – been attacking originality and beginnings. It's rather like those people who hold that the universe is all middle. It doesn't really matter how it originated, and it may go on for an infinitude of time. I'm putting words in your mouth, but I wonder if you accept them.

PE: Yes, you are very good at that. I often use the same strategy. ⊅

Swanke Hayden Connell Architects

New York Times Building
Temporary Marketing Office

Near Manhattan's garment district, a marketing suite has been built expressly to sear designer Renzo Piano's forthcoming Times skyscraper 'early and indelibly' in the imaginations of New Yorkers. **Craig Kellogg** explains how the local practice of Swanke Hayden Connell Architects combined classic contemporary furniture with native New York minimalist detailing to embody the humanistic Modernism of an Italian master.

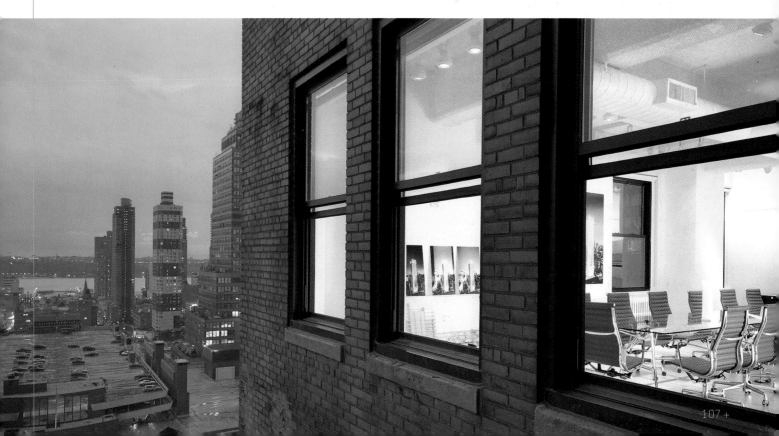

Times Square was named for the *New York Times*, so owners
of the newspaper were unlikely to stray far from their familiar
mid-Manhattan stomping ground to build a new headquarters
tower. After a search, the paper settled on down-at-heels
redevelopment land across from the teeming Port Authority
bus terminal, on the ragged edge of the city's garment district.
By contrast the building proposed by Renzo Piano for the site
was a shimmering vision in white. And despite lavish media
coverage heralding its arrival on the horizon, a vision it
remains today. Literally there is no building yet. In fact, the
only tangible bits of the Times tower actually in evidence at
present are drawings and models produced by Piano with New
York City firm Fox & Fowle.

Of course it's necessary that a landmark skyscraper in
Manhattan be established early and indelibly in the public
imagination. A skyscraper's image is probably its most
important feature. Unbuilt icons are especially appealing to
the architecture elite, where there can be unlimited
enthusiasm for paper architecture. But paper architecture
generally doesn't sell, which vexes developers needing to
market new buildings well before they come online. In the case
of the Times tower, the need is especially pressing because
land costs have prompted developer Forest City Ratner to plan
about twice as much space as the Times company will actually
fill. To dispose of the excess, an increasingly common interiors
typology comes to the rescue: the temporary marketing office.

Effective marketing facilities conjure the product they sell in
detail. When architecture is a major selling point for a project,
these suites play a key role in communicating the design. They
must stoke the fantasy that will transport roomfuls of hard-
boiled business types into a future five years hence, when a
tower will be complete and companies are moving in.

To begin, Ratner engaged and combined two small rooms in
an ordinary masonry bloc adjacent to the building site. Visitors
enter the space from an unappealing common corridor with
low ceilings and unpleasant fluorescent lighting. But, inside,

Below
Piano and Fox & Fowle's planned New York Times building, shown in the context
of other Manhattan skyscrapers – nestling among the golden towers.

common lay-in acoustic ceiling panels have been mostly banished, to restore a welcome sense of space and light under old-fashioned tall ceilings.

Essentially, the mood takes converted downtown industrial lofts for inspiration. Senior designer Agatha Rady, of Swanke Hayden Connell Architects, zoned the flowing scheme with sliding doors, which usually remain open. Marketing functions peel off of the foyer gallery, which displays bulky architectural models. The large, adjacent meeting room overlooks the tower site below. The smaller conference room offers a slightly different vantage on the same scene (now a car park and low buildings which will be demolished). An alcove serves support staff and provides a small pantry.

Classic New York minimalist detailing frames newly revealed bones and beams throughout. Ductwork is artfully exposed. But having discarded the acoustic ceilings, noise was a concern. So hard ceilings are textured with sprayed Pyrok soundproofing. The floors, which look like wood strips, are in fact prefinished Wood-o-cork laminate planks from Wicanders. Usually seen in high-traffic areas like shopping centres, they have the advantage of muting footsteps, which are often unbearably loud in lofts with traditional wood floors.

To furnish these rooms, Rady leaned heavily on serious, timeless pieces by major players in the history of modern design. Modular storage and desks are from USM Haller Systems. The NOMOS table is a favourite designed by Lord Norman Foster. And Eames executive chairs are from the experimental aluminium group. But red leather upholstery is the 21st-century architectural equivalent of the 1980s power necktie, a sophisticated note of humour.

Now several months into its projected five-year life (which ends, presumably, when the tower opens) the marketing offices succeed in communicating Piano's architectural vision for upscale, humanistic Modernism. His deep and continuing commitment to quality design and construction would surprise few Europeans. But it is a message that must be made explicit and continually justified to visiting members of the tight-fisted real estate community in New York. The unfamiliar ingredient in the Times tower is money. Indeed, Rady also persuaded Ratner to spend more than originally planned for fitting out the marketing space. You can't fake quality. Exceptional design is separated from regular building by an unexpectedly fine line. A few subtle details and straightforward decisions, carefully executed, transform a place not-so-great into something else. That is the success of Rady's marketing offices. And now it is Piano's challenge on the site next door. Δ

OCEAN NORTH

Tuuli Sotamaa   Kivi Sotamaa   Birger Sevaldson   Michael Hensel

OCEAN NORTH is a Helsinki-based practice that undertakes projects, research and consultancy in architecture, urban design, product design and cultural production. Tuuli Sotamaa, Kivi Sotamaa, Birger Sevaldson and Michael Hensel lead the firm's investigations of synergetic relations across design disciplines and scales – from small-scale products to architecture and urban design. **Christopher Hight** examines their work as a form of practice that resists a profile.

A practice profile would seem focused around the first term. The reader expects a description of a firm, a singular genius or corporate body. To provide this, the writer traces themes across individual projects, finding a consistency of thought, process, trope, or technique. Indeed, it is the explicit task of the writer to uncover a continuity that binds isolated works to a coherent 'practice', a corpus of work, an oeuvre. As such, the practice profile is similar to 'auteur theory' of film studies. They both suggest their respective practices are too complex, require too many specialities and are far too contingent upon exterior forces (budgets, clients, etc) for an authorial vision to be fully realised in any single work. Only by examining a series of projects can a distinctive authorship be established.

However, we have already shifted from the 'practice' to the issue of the 'profile', that is, the representation which identifies an author as such. The task before us hinges around not the first empirical term but this second, theoretical, problem.

To what extent is tracing such a portrait of a firm like drawing a profile of a face? In the late 18th century, drawing silhouetted profiles became a popular pastime within the most fashionable Parisian salons. The subject sat parallel to a screen and a candle projected his or her shadow upon it; this outline was then traced as a single line that supposedly revealed otherwise hidden traits of the sitter. While revealing latent character is a common theme of European portraiture, the profile is a special case. Firstly, it did not seek a naturalistic resemblance but abstracted the face into a continuous contour to be read and deciphered as a text; the formal attributes of this line were thought to express the content latent within the soul of the subject. Secondly, drawing profiles was not simply a diversionary pleasure but also a tool of subjectification. It was central to the 'sciences' of criminal anthropology and physiognomy, and to this day police, immigration and intelligence agencies use 'profiling' to identify potential threats. These profiles operate forensically (like a finger print, a retinal scan or a DNA test) to define a suspect subject to the gaze of the police – or the critic. In AD, long one of the most fashionable salons for architecture, the practice

profile offers a similar forum to identify what a contemporary practice signifies. One evening, we draw a paper screen between our object and ourselves and upon that translucent white surface trace a shadowy line along which we search for the significance of the author.

All this would be a long digression except that such a profile depends upon certain preconditions; namely, the possibility of drawing a contour, and therefore of a necessarily bounded, hierarchical, whole, and unified organic order. We profile faces, not amoebas, humanist subjects, not rhizomes nor networks. On reflection it is clear that the type of authorship a practice profile depends upon is a set of a priori values that amounts to nothing else than a Vitruvian system applied not to geometry but to the forms and order of practice.

Yet the significance of OCEAN NORTH – like that of an elite of other young firms – ultimately lies in its promise of a non-Vitruvian formation of practice. Or rather, given its explicit desire to formulate alternative modes of working, we can understand the firm not on the grounds of consistency or coherence but on how they comply to or resist the profile.

In 1995, Ocean Net emerged from the Architectural Association's nascent graduate design programme. It was an association of small, semi-autonomous practices located across Europe as an attempt to think – or rather, work – through the problem of how a group of young, likeminded architects could forge a significant practice under today's professional limitations. A network organisation would allow each node to remain highly adaptive yet able to pool resources for competitions and larger projects. As Gregory Bateson stated, a network remains local at all points however extensive, and the Ocean Net was to operate upon the specific cultural and economic milieus of its individual nodes while engaging broader issues with global effects. Theirs was not and is not a 'critical'

Top
Formations: Surfaces.

Bottom left
Formations: Furniture.

Bottom right
Formations: Objects.

Formations Installation
Commissioned by the Fondazione Nicola Trussardi
Milan, 2002
The Formations Installation consists of an interior space with integrated
furniture and objects. Two sets of horizontal surfaces – one raised from the
floor and another suspended from the ceiling – articulate a fluid spatial
movement in the Trussardi gallery. Furniture is integrated into their fluid
arrangement according to the same formal logic. Where the furniture surfaces
undulate they provide seating. Likewise, surfaces are articulated to receive
objects nested within these deformations. The installation was fabricated
through computer-aided manufacturing; the furniture was produced by CNC-
milling, and the objects via rapid prototyping that allowed highly articulated
hollow containers that can be appropriated as tableware, lighting devices and
containers for storage. Extensive digital and analogue modelling was employed
to develop a varied yet coherent articulation of all material elements further
enriched by dynamic light and sound. The result is a vigorous, immersive
environment that challenges the visitor to engage with space in an inventive
manner and which emphasises the dynamic processes of Formation.

Below
Exhibition architecture for the ARS 01 international Art Exhibition
at KIASMA-Museum of Contemporary Art, Helsinki, Finland, 2001.
Left: Fifth Floor; Right: Digital Model.

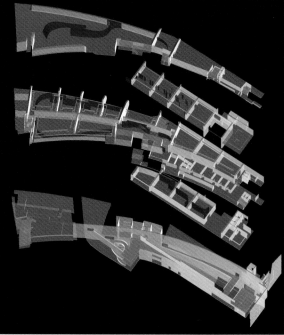

deconstruction of architecture nor a post-1968 radicalism in which architecture should burn. Instead, they sought to reclaim and conserve a positive and projective role for their discipline (although this meant widening its borders).

As with so many of the avant-gardes of the 20th century, this ambitious association was extremely volatile and this united design web lasted only a few years, suggesting the difficulty underlying rhetoric of a smoothly networked society. They may also have inscribed its goals too literally into a structure that was inherently conflicted. OCEAN NORTH precipitated out of the dissolution of Ocean Net but rather than understand it as a tattered remnant or retreat it is more useful to understand how it has internalised its progenitor's goals.

Firstly, the practice is trans-disciplinary and multi-modal. The partners, Tuuli and Kivi Sotamaa, Birger Sevaldson and Michael Hensel, are an international collective of diverse disciplines and interests from urbanism to ceramics and from digital technologies to structural innovation. They closely collaborate with a wide spectrum of imminent experts from relevant fields. This pragmatic and multidisciplinary approach – which they liken to industrial design more than architecture – employs contradictory processes of formation to design room-sized installation, building design, furniture, small objects, or even websites. Moreover, their use of digital tools consciously attempts to incorporate anterior architectural concerns of budget, clients and site, as well as posterior issues of use and performance. They also teach and research. In fact, OCEAN NORTH serves as a condenser for all these activities since it attempts to see each project and commission as an opportunity for serious design research.

Secondly, the practice is geographically distributed. The collaborators often communicate across the North Sea (hence the name?) and half of the projects are generated from Oslo and London. The rest emerge from their main office in Helsinki. Within this Finnish context, OCEAN NORTH engages and offers an alternative to what has become the burdensome legacy of Alto and phenomenology. This confrontation became

direct in their recent exhibit design, ARS 01, at Steven Holl's KIASMA-museum. Rather than respecting the existing building or attempting to insert a disruption to Holl's architecture, OCEAN NORTH pursued a transformative approach that subtly altered the spatial and visual effects of the existing architecture. Often it is difficult to determine where Holl's building ends and OCEAN NORTH's installation began. This formal and performative affiliation extended to the relationship between the works on display as their design inflected to the traits and needs of each work.

This affiliative tactic is the third significant trait of their practice. In an earlier project, the Extraterrain, a topological surface mapped the human body in the way that ARS 01 mapped Holl's architecture. If ARS 01 challenged the phenomenological sensibility of the existing architecture, the Extraterrain questioned our habitual postures and furniture typologies, drawing attention to the relationship between the body and space as a post-ergonomic playground. Their most recent project, the Formations Installation at the Fondazione Nicola Trussardi in Milan, synthesises both the ergonomic performativity of the Extraterrain and the formal-visual effects of ARS 01. Rather than pursue a fantasy of seamless merger between architecture and furniture or repeat a Modernist dialectic, OCEAN NORTH deploys a choreographed reciprocity across architectural surfaces (they are not classical walls or floors), ergonomic surfaces (likewise, not typological furniture), discrete events (or rather the interaction between objects and their display) and human bodies (again, supposedly non-Vitruvian). This project also

Top
World Center: View from Manhattan.

Bottom left
World Center: Circulation Diagram.

Bottom right
World Center: Elevations.

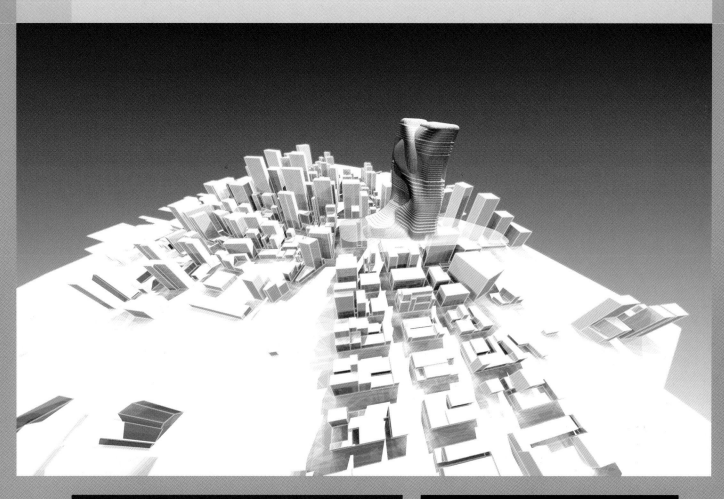

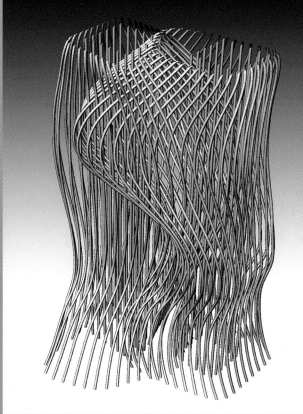

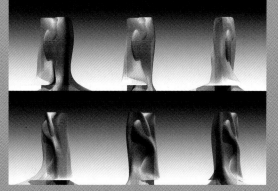

World Center for Human Concerns
Commissioned by the Max Protetch Gallery
for the 'A New World Trade Center' Exhibition
New York, 2001

OCEAN NORTH'S design for a World Center for Human Concerns on the former site of the World Trade Center in Manhattan proposes a space for all peoples and cultures, whether established or emerging. At this stage, no detailed programme or spatial requirements were appropriate. Instead, their scheme projects an architecture appropriate for emergent and temporal social and institutional organisations.

In part a memorial to the drama of 11 September 2001, the new World Center inscribes itself around the volume of the previous Twin Towers, which remain visible as voided figures through the textured and folded skins of the new building. Spatial differentiation is articulated via material differentiation of the building skin (as opposed to the traditional strategy of vertical zoning). Moreover, the design is purposefully ambiguous and can be read either as a single object folded upon itself or as two objects entwined in conflict or fusion. There is no privileged viewpoint from which the design can be understood in its entirety, and the tension between blankness and diversity, continuity and differentiation suggests a baroque relationship between the object and the beholder.

Top left
Landsc[r]aper: Circulation and programmatic diagrams.

Middle
Landsc[r]aper: Urban ring organisation.

Bottom
Landsc[r]aper: Digital model of proposal.

Top right
Landsc[r]aper: Urban organisation diagram.

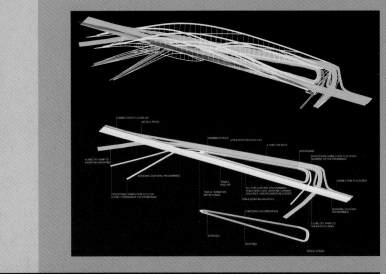

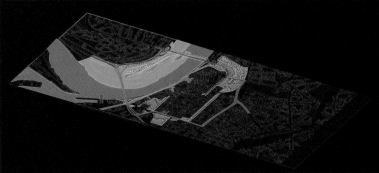

Landsc[r]aper Urban Ring Bridge
Commissioned by the NRW Forum for Culture and Economy
for the 'Living Bridge' Exhibition
Duesseldorf, 2000
OCEAN NORTH's proposal for the Landsc[r]aper Urban Ring Bridge argues that an inhabitable bridge is only viable when it intensively engages the surrounding urban condition. Connectivity, programmatic intensification and projected performance are therefore central to their scheme, which attempts to extend existing organisational and demographic structures and is affiliated with a set of programmatic and infrastructural rings that already exist within the city, including the seasonally usable floodplain of the river and the promenades on both sides.

The design strategy condenses and bundles programmatic and infrastructural trajectories to induce various types of movement, allow different populations to interact and sustain the diverse urban condition of inner Düsseldorf. This diversity is further articulated and entrained through geometrically varied arch and beam structures and moveable building skins. Additionally, the differentiated geometry of the structure offers a set of effects that enhance orientation when moving through this very large and complex structure. Through an assemblage of related structural systems and material envelopes, the bridge introduces a dynamic landmark to Düsseldorf that reflects the heterogeneous, dynamic and progressive culture of the city and its inner-urban infrastructural landscape.

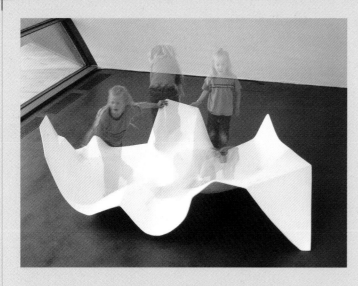

brings together research on furnishing, installations and object fabrication. Likewise, in their recent project for a time capsule, a_drift, the sensuous forms of the container derive from the mass and shape of objects contained therein. At the time of the competition, these contents were unspecified so OCEAN NORTH employed computer animation software to develop a parametric design that could adapt the forms of each capsule to whatever might be contained. This approach was then deployed at a far larger scale for their competition entry for the World Center for Human Concerns, in which sinuous envelopes were configured to wrap a void where the minimalist towers of the World Trade Center once stood. Such affiliative design stresses the dynamic relations between subject and built environment as an opportunity to articulate social and cultural organisation. As their projects increasingly shift from more or less temporary architectures and speculative projects to more permanent and extensive built structures, it will be interesting to see how more traditional building programmes might be transformed through similarly affiliative approaches. The question is open as to whether a firm can sustain this contra-Vitruvian approach or whether it will coalesce into a different sort of brand or signature.

If tactics of affiliation are OCEAN NORTH's recurrent design approach, by its very nature this is not a unified strategy but rather a set of tactical operations in dispersion and transformation. Such a firm's profile lies not within a single coherent line but along multiple muting trajectories of opportunistic abstraction. ⌂

Christopher Hight is a theorist and designer teaching at the Architectural Association Design Research Laboratory. He has been a Fulbright Scholar and has received other awards, including the AIA School Medal. He has practised in the United States and as a member of the Renzo Piano Building Workshop, and has published in America and Europe. He is currently completing a doctoral thesis on the role of measure, the body and cybernetics in post-Second World War architecture and urbanism.

Summary Resumé

1995	Ocean Net was founded
1995–98	Various collaborative projects including Töölö Open Arena and the Chamberworks Installation
1998	OCEAN NORTH is founded as a merger between the OCEAN nodes in Helsinki, Oslo and Cologne
1999	a_drift Time capsules
	Invited Design Competition by the New York Times, New York, USA
	Finalist Entry
2000	Intencities
	Installation at ArtGenda 2000
	Commissioned by the ArtGenda Office – Baltic Region Young Artists Biennial, Helsinki, Finland
2000	Landsc[r]aper – Urban Ringbridge
	Design study for the 'Living Bridges' exhibition
	Commissioned by the NRW Forum for Culture and Economy, Düsseldorf, Germany
2000	Ambient Amplifiers
	FEIDAD Competition Entry, Taipei, Taiwan
	Finalist Entry
2000	Narva Masterplan
	Pre-masterplan study
	Commissioned by the Narva City Planning Office, Narva, Estonia
2001	d-Fusion Seminar and Exhibition
	hosted by OCEAN NORTH and NIFCA (Nordic Institute of Contemporary Art) in Helsinki, Finland
2001	ARS 01
	Exhibition Architecture for the ARS 01 international Art Exhibition at KIASMA
	Commissioned by KIASMA-Museum of Contemporary Art, Helsinki, Finland
2001	World Center for Human Concerns
	Design Study for the 'A new World Trade Center' Exhibition
	Commissioned by the Max Protetch Gallery, New York, USA
2002	Do-group Session 2002 – The Space of Extremes
	hosted by OCEAN NORTH in Helsinki, Finland
2002	OCEAN NORTH exhibits work in the 'Mood River' exhibition at the Wexner Center of the Arts, Columbus, Ohio
2002	Ionic.nifca.org
	Design for a Virtual Gallery for the exhibition of digital art
	Commissioned by NIFCA
2002	Formations
	Installation with integrated Furniture and Object Design
	Commissioned by the Fondazione Nicola Trussardi, Milan, Italy

About the Partners

Tuuli Sotamaa studied ceramics and glass design at the University of Art and Design in Helsinki (UIAH), and industrial design at the Central Saint Martins College of Graphics and Industrial Design. Her portfolio includes artworks, installation and exhibition design, industrial design and material research. She has worked for Alessi FAO spa in Italy and currently teaches workshops at the Institute for Industrial Design at the Oslo School of Architecture. She is also a founding member of the do-group.

Kivi Sotamaa studied spatial and furniture design at the University of Art and Design in Helsinki (UIAH), and architecture at the Helsinki University of Technology (HUT). He pursues PhD research at the Future Home Institute at UIAH, lectures widely in Europe and the US, is a founding member of the do-group, and has taught in various schools of architecture and design in Europe.

Birger Sevaldson is an interior architect and designer working in a broad field. A founding member of the do-group, he is Associate Professor at the Institute for Industrial Design in Oslo and Vice Rector of the Oslo School of Architecture.

Michael Hensel is an architect, Unit Master of Diploma Unit 4 and Course-organiser of the post-professional Emergent Technologies and Design Programme at the Architectural Association School of Architecture in London. He is also a founding member of the do-group.

Energy in Use

**RUTHERFORD INFORMATION SERVICES CENTRE,
GOLDSMITHS COLLEGE, LONDON**
Architect: Allies and Morrison
Even on the north facade, natural light has to be thought about
carefully so that computers can be used inside without disabling
reflections from the monitors. This full-height glazing enables the
light to penetrate deep into the space. The surplus heat from the use
of the building is removed by ventilation air which runs continuously
and delivers air under the floor. As the daytime heats up, heat inside
the building is absorbed by the heavy coffered precast ceiling without
the building becoming uncomfortably hot.

Following on from last issue's article on embodied energy by Gil Friend and Bob Reed, **Max Fordham** investigates building emissions. Establishing first what is meant by the loose use of the term 'energy', he highlights why in the West about half of all emissions are now caused by buildings. He tackles which are the key parts of the metabolism of a building that can be tailored to minimise the rejection or admittance of excess energy. He illustrates his points with some of the buildings that he and his practice have collaborated on.

We all use the word energy a bit loosely. The idea of energy crystallised in the 18th century with the realisation that heat which raised the temperature of things and energy of movement were equivalent.

That is to say, you could completely convert all the energy of movement into heat. It was discovered that it is more difficult to convert heat into movement. If you started with a certain amount of heat, you could convert some into work, but there would be heat left over. However, the amount of leftover heat added to the amount of movement energy was equal to the amount of heat at the start of the process.

There are various names for movement energy: work, kinetic energy, potential energy, and electrical energy.

In all conversions of one kind of energy to another, the starting energy and the finishing energy are the same. Energy is conserved in processes, it cannot be used up or lost. Energy can be measured, and the measure of energy is called the joule. It takes 4200 joules to heat 1 kilogram of water through 1°C and 10 joules to raise 1 kilogram through a metre of height against the force of gravity. To heat a kettle of water, say, 0.5 kilograms from 10°C from a cold tap to 100°C boiling in 2 minutes or 120 seconds requires:

4200 x 0.5 x (100 – 10) = 189,000 joules in 120 seconds or 1600 joules in 1 second.

A joule per second is called a watt, and 1000 joules per second is a kilowatt.

There is a hierarchy of types of energy. In the case of heat, the hierarchy is defined by the temperature. Heat can only flow from a hot place to a cooler one.

The sun is very hot – millions of degrees Centigrade – and by way of mirrors it can be used to melt steel. For example, there are solar furnaces in Spain. However, after sunlight has been degraded by clouds, it cannot be focused in a solar furnace.

Light from the sun is the origin of almost everything that happens on earth. It generates photosynthesis and makes plants grow. The earth is at a temperature where the heat it radiates to the cold universe is equal to the heat received from the sun. It was realised towards the end of the 19th century that if the earth were solid its temperature would be much too cold for life to exist. The atmosphere acts as a screen which allows light to reach the earth but, because of the carbon dioxide content, inhibits the radiation outward of the long-wave infrared rays. Arrhenius calculated the effect of the known amount of carbon dioxide in the atmosphere.

Solar energy is at its strongest at the equator and weakest at the poles, but the energy is radiated away from the earth as a whole. This means energy has to be transported from the equator to the poles, and the weather and ocean currents provide the means of transport. The overall pattern of the weather is very mixed up with cyclones, anticyclones, rain and frosts.

Plants take light energy and use it to combine carbon dioxide and water to make cellulose, plant material, and sugar. Mostly this process is reversed when the plants decompose, but over the lifecycle of the earth a very small amount has been incorporated in the earth's crust as fossil fuel. The rate of laying down fossil fuel is very small – about the same rate as running a single electric kettle – but we use this fossil fuel at a considerably higher rate.

The population of the world might stabilise at 10 billion people if the progress of industrialisation is spread beyond the one billion people who currently have access to the industrialised use of fossil fuel. So there is a potential ten-fold increase in the use of fossil fuel and production of carbon dioxide if we do not change our pattern of energy use.

In a highly developed Western economy, about half the emissions are caused by buildings. This includes all the fuel burnt in power stations to make the electricity used in buildings as well as all the heat for heating and hot water.

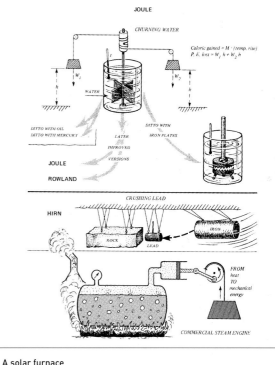

These drawings from a school physics textbook for Year 4 showing an experiment by Joule which churns water, crushing lead, and a commercial steam engine, illustrate how heat and energy of movement are equivalent.

A solar furnace

When the object is at the same temperature as the sun it radiates the same ammount of heat to the sun as it receives.

Energy flows on earth

	billion kW	Tons C/sec
solar radiation reaching the earth	150,000	
use of fossil fuel now	39	700
use of fossil fuel with 10 billion people on earth	390	7,000
total photosynthesis	1,650	25,000
average rate of fossil fuel production	2/1,000,000,000	
which is	2kW	

Pattern of energy use

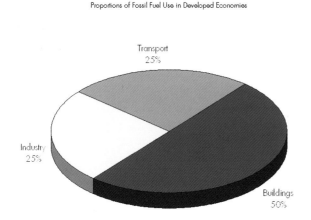

Proportions of Fossil Fuel Use in Developed Economies

Transport
25%

Industry
25%

Buildings
50%

About a quarter is used for transport. Of course this is growing as the price of air travel falls and we travel all over the earth. Travel to work is significant, and we should be planning cities and the means of production to reduce the demand for transport.

The remaining quarter is used for production. I am always surprised by this low proportion. It could be distorted by the economic fact of exporting heavy production to underdeveloped economies – production has to be concerned with this aspect of carbon emission. Packing seems an unnecessary part of production. However, the construction industry has a direct impact on the main part of carbon emission, and we need to examine where the energy goes and see what can be done to reduce the energy flow.

One of the most important points to remember is that there is a very wide variation in use even between apparently similar buildings. So it is quite likely that for a large development of identical flats the ratio of the maximum to the minimum energy bill is 6. This variation caused by the wide variety of human behaviour masks the variation due to aspects like insulation of the walls. It also means that a large factor in the reduction of carbon emissions is management of installations. This includes maintenance throughout the life of those installations and continued monitoring of the way they are used.

In addition, design needs to address some of the key variables, such as how to provide plenty of ventilation without wasting energy, and we also need to examine the use of light very carefully.

Having said this we must also understand how the energy that is supplied to a building is used before it flows outside as warm air, conducted through the envelope of the building, and a little as warm drainage.

The breakdown of use depends on the use of the building. Houses which are usually dimly lit take in energy for heating, a little for lighting and some for heating water for domestic use. Air-conditioning is seldom used.

In buildings where people work, a bright environment is

expected, so electricity for light represents about half of the carbon emissions. Then mechanical ventilation and air-conditioning may be necessary to reject the heat that gets into the building. Electricity to run the equipment in the building supplements the heat needed to maintain a comfortable winter temperature.

The next issue is the predominance of existing buildings. While we can hope to improve the design of new buildings, the major problem is upgrading those that are already in existence.

Buildings are like animals – they have a metabolism of heat that is produced inside. The heat has many sources:

People
We each produce about 100W, ie 100 Joules/second per person, plus some heat as moisture.

Equipment
The equipment we use – computers, cookers, freezers, TV, factory machinery.

Light
Natural light is about
1W per 100 lumens.

If we filter out the infra red it becomes
0.5W per 100 lumens.

Fluorescent light is also about
1W of electricity per 100 lumens

although this become about
3W per 100 lumens(of fuel in a power station)

Incandescent light is about
10W of electricity or 30W of fossil fuel per 100 lumens.

The heat released inside a building has to be able to flow out of the building, and the building has to be kept comfortable. The part of a building with direct contact with the outside exchanges energy with the outside. If we could design a building so that the internal metabolism

HAILEYBURY SCHOOL POOL, HERTFORD
Architect: Studio E Architects
Overheating in a swimming pool is not usually a problem in the UK but it is important to manage the ventilation so that the humidity can be limited without an excessive amount of air needing to be heated up. Natural lighting comes into its own here and the electric lighting can be run at a low level at night.

offset the heat loss on the coldest day, then for all warmer days heat has to be rejected.

Heat can be rejected by controlling the ventilation. As the outside temperature rises, it gets so hot inside that the heat cannot be removed by ventilation during the day. However, at night cool air can remove the heat and then during the day excess heat can flow into the solid surfaces of a room. In fact all the metabolism in a room occurs at random times.

The temperature of a room is evened out over 24 hours and, with a well-insulated building with a large surface area of solid material facing into the room, it is possible to maintain a 24-hour stable temperature. This is called using thermal mass.

An internal part of a building also has its metabolism. To get heat to flow to surrounding rooms, the central rooms have to be hotter than the surrounding rooms. They cannot all be comfortable. So the central rooms need some circulatory system of cool water or air. Basically this defines an air-conditioning system.

In the LT Method, the passive zones with direct contact to the outside should be maximised while the internal zones waste energy on mechanical systems to remove their internal energy.

One of the key parts of the metabolism of a building is the energy for lighting. In a house, satisfactory lighting (50 to 100 lux) for a 10 metres squared room is represented by a window of about 20 per cent of the floor area.

For a space where people work, much higher light levels are expected, so electric lighting of 500 to 1000 lux or large windows and roof lights are needed.

The amount of light provided in a building is one of the key determinants for energy use.

As the light level required increases, window size has to be increased and/or there is an increase of electrical energy needed for lighting. In addition, the increased window area leads to an increased heat loss and heating load in cold weather. At the same time there is an increased summer cooling load. So as the demand for light rises, the energy use of a building will also rise.

This discussion also shows why building space should be able to be coupled to the outside. In the LT Method, passive space is the term used to define naturally lit space which can also be ventilated naturally.

The whole issue of the requirement for light is very important and subtle. The requirement for natural light has built up by evolution and historical precedent. The end result is that natural lighting provides a daylight factor of around 0.5 per cent to 2 per cent. This represents 25 to 100 lux on an overcast day. As electric light sources increased in efficiency and research into seeing was developed, design light levels for offices peaked at about 1000 lux in the early 1970s. Now the

Double cube room by Inigo Jones, Wilton House, Wiltshire. An example of the way storey heights were increased in the 17th century to optimise on natural light.

consensus has reduced to about 300 to 500 lux as a result of the 1973 OPEC oil crisis and the current anxiety about global warming.

A 10 per cent daylight factor on an overcast day is represented by 500 lux, and it is impossible to achieve this level of daylighting from a window in a low, deep room. It is clear that the electric lights are used almost all the time in daylit offices which are, say, 6 metres deep and a bit under 3 metres high. To achieve good natural light, storey heights have to be increased to be about equal to the depth of a room, as in the grand houses of the 17th century. Alternatively, roof lights can be used.

These large windows bring thermal problems. If they are sized to give good light on an overcast day then bright sunlight brings 20 times more light and energy. During hot or even mild weather, the space will become too hot. The excess of heat must be rejected. Shading by awnings, shades, shutters, blinds or curtains is the traditional solution, and this needs to be reinvented for the 21st century. High-technology ideas such as electrochromic or photochromic glass may also satisfy the requirement.

Fixed shades exclude overcast light and make it more difficult to provide adequate light on an overcast day, so shading should be provided and controlled automatically to admit or exclude solar energy according to demand.

In cold weather the large windows are an energy benefit when they admit useful light, ie when the space is occupied and it is daytime. At other times, mainly at night, but also when the light is dim and the room unoccupied, the windows are losing heat and need an insulating cover. Shutters and heavy curtains were used for insulation in the 19th century, but now we use them mainly to give privacy at night.

During hot weather the internal metabolism of energy has to be rejected to ventilation at night. This requirement leads to a need to design openings (the reason for using windows is worth discussing) that can allow ventilation at night without posing a security risk and without causing disturbance inside the room.

Security problems lead to a demand for roller shutters, and these can provide shading and insulation.

So the design starts with a choice of light level. Then storey height and glazed area are fixed to provide proper light on an overcast day. Controllable shutters to provide insulation, control of daylight and security are then designed.

Finally, thermal mass and provision for ventilation can be chosen.

New buildings should be designed with intelligent, controllable provision for natural light and natural ventilation.

The indoor cricket school at Lord's, London. (Architect: David Morley Architects) This unheated building has roof lighting to 1200 lux on an overcast day for playing indoor cricket. A barrel-vaulted roof profile was developed to allow north light to enter. Fabric blinds diffuse the light and prevent the penetration of direct sunlight. During the daytime, electric lights are kept off.

Diagram of the design process

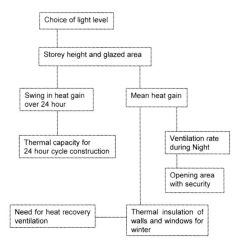

New heating based on mechanical ventilation with heat reclaim allows generous ventilation rates without wasting energy. Of course incandescent lights must be replaced with efficient light sources.

When all these things have been done and the demand for energy has been reduced by around 80 per cent, then we have the opportunity to supply buildings from renewable sources such as windmills and tidal barrages – even photovoltaic cells might have a place. ∆

A number of adjustments are needed to bring the existing housing stock up to standard. Windows need to be replaced, fitted with insulated automated shades and automatic ventilation. Walls need to be insulated, and this is likely to mean covering brick buildings with insulating material and a finish detailed to look like traditional stucco.

Max Fordham is the founding partner of building services engineers Max Fordham LLP. Established in London in 1966, the firm now has a staff of over 100 engineers and administrators. The practice specialises in the relationship of building form to electrical and mechanical services. It aims to design sustainable buildings that also achieve the highest BREEAM rating by reducing energy consumption for heating and lighting, obviating air-conditioning and by careful selection of materials. The office's skills in designing energy-efficient systems have been recognised with numerous awards.

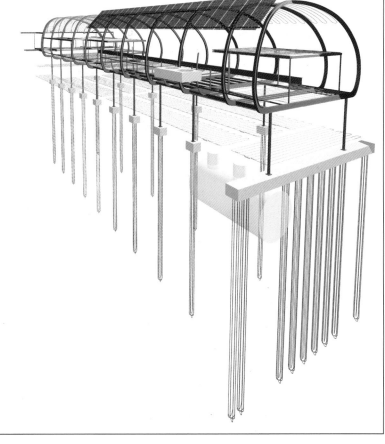

ST GEORGES MEWS, LONDON
Architect: Paxton Locher Architects
This combined commercial office and residential building is on a very restricted town site. Rooflights provide generous lighting with very efficient double glazing with low emissivity glass and argon fill. Automatic metalised roller blinds are controlled to capture solar heat in the winter and to reflect it in the summer when it is not required. The metalised roller blinds are closed during a winter's night to reduce the heat loss from the windows to a low level. During summer, heat can be rejected to the ground under the building using pipes cast into the pile foundations and during the winter heat is extracted from the ground and used to heat the building.

Vénissieux Mediatheques

Jeremy Melvin describes a modest media centre that Dominique Perrault, the architect of the Bibliothèque de France, has built for a Lyons satellite town. In so doing, Melvin accounts for not only Perrault's response to a small-scale urban context but also to a burgeoning building type that has already occupied the likes of Norman Foster and Toyo Ito (see Δ, vol 71, no 5).

Mediatheques, the contributions of Norman Foster and Toyo Ito to the genre notwithstanding, are, like the word, undoubtably a French invention, rather as Boullee and Ledoux left the seminal images of libraries. And Foster's was, after all, at Nîmes in the south of France. Between 1980 and 2001 almost two thousand municipal libraries were built in France as local politicians took advantage of increased powers, took note of the Centre Pompidou's embryonic example of a multimedia information centre, and took umbrage at the poor provision of library services relative to Germany or the UK. As so often in French history the response to a perceived problem is to create a systematic institution, and given the strength of precedent it was almost inevitable that architecture would become the visible symbol of its solution.

If Nîmes set the precedent, the trend has trickled into decreasingly glamorous settings, although in many cases the architecture has remained of a high quality. Among the examples of this phenomenon is Dominique Perrault's mediatheque in Vénissieux, a town within the Lyons conglomeration. Unlike some Lyons satellites, Vénissieux is known for its notorious housing estates like Les Minguettes, rather than the number of Michelin stars awarded to its restaurants.

In location it may be a world away from Perrault's best-known building, the Bibliothèque de France, but given its compatible function there is some purpose in the familial similarities. And its population does have a very high proportion of young people, precisely the

target group for the wave of public libraries. Indeed, in a country where every schoolchild of the same age – including those in the overseas *départements* – is reputed to follow the same lesson at any given time, there is a consistency in scholars in the national library experiencing a similar architecture to immigrants in depressed townships.

With its bold, glazed forms and finely controlled relationship with a formalised surrounding landscape, the Vénissieux mediatheque is recognisably from the same stable as the *tres grand bibliothèque*. But there is one difference which speaks volumes about the way Perrault's apparently cold and rational architecture can adapt to specific circumstances. Having decided to locate the books at the Bibliothèque de France in the four L-shaped corner towers, he faced the challenge of shading them from the sun. One rumoured possible solution was to finish the glass with the gold relief that coats astronauts' visors. The cost was apparently prohibitive even to the project's sponsor, President François Mitterrand, a man with few other discernible signs of thrift – though had the first men on the moon been French rather than American it may have appealed to his patriotic sense of duty.

At Vénissieux there was no chance for similar profligacy. Instead his solution for the glass-clad building is much more subtle and contributes positively to the overall architectural concept. It was to introduce a sheet of perforated metal between the two leaves of glass. This deceptively simple solution is more or less universal: it works equally well on south-facing walls as solar shading, and does not compromise energy saving measures on the north. Lending the facades, especially at the distance, the look of a stack of data servers or filing cabinets, it also makes an appropriate trope of the building's function, capturing the inherent ambiguity of a mediatheque where access to information in any form, not just on the printed page, is the defining purpose. Glinting mysteriously in sunlight, the interplay between metal and glass evokes an enigmatic feel, reinforced by the different though complementary characteristics of these two materials used together in such an unusual way. And finally, this all-round screen-like facade helps to define the architectural concept by creating a circulation zone between it and the reading areas, an interstitial space which offers limited views out, almost as if through heavy rain, or access to the information.

Perrault's architecture achieves its power through an uncanny ability to identify the single bold gesture which

Below left
Ground floor plan. All the public areas are on one floor, though an
asymmetrically placed concourse divides it into one zone for young
children and another for adults and teenagers. This contains general
information desks, services and access to the offices above. It also
functions as a form of public space with the reading area simulating the
private realm. Within the two reading areas are various spaces for
conventional library use, computers and other forms of media, though
organised without an obvious hierarchy. All around is the perimeter ring
behind the facade.

Below right
Sections. The long section in particular reveals the industrial-like construction of
the building. With large areas of column-free space the mediatheque can adapt to
perhaps unforeseen changes in information delivery and management, though it
also suggests the transience of any given taxonomy of knowledge and implies
intellectual freedom for individuals.

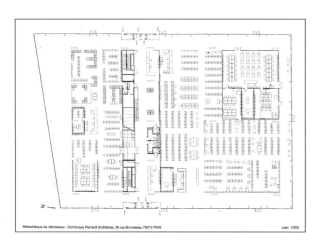

responds evocatively to physical and perceptual context, and
this is as true of the overall form as the facade. Its precinct is
levelled to blend with the neighbouring streets, its public areas
are all at ground level. The four-storey slab protruding above
the podium contains administrative offices, and marks, at
ground level, the entrance and public spine which divides the
children's from the adults' areas. Together with the perimeter
ring, this concourse provides the semblance of public urban
space within the building, while the individual desks and
workstations resemble private spheres. Inside the building
assumes an industrial character, with steel trusses and hard
floor, while the timber bookstacks and reading desks lend
warmth and and create a more intimate scale.

The pattern of internal organisation is the kernel of a series
of interventions within the immediate context. Two defining
characteristics of the area are its low-density development and
ample planting, yet, explains Perrault, many of the advantages
this could bring are compromised by insensitive planning.
Marcel Houel Avenue, for example, divides the two urban
blocks which make up the site, justifying his aim 'to create a
street landscape that merges nature and architecture'.

The analogies between building and town are subtle and
sophisticated. As the mediatheque has a dividing axis, so the
town's organisation hinges around the junction of two
perpendicular avenues. Just as readers in the mediatheque

can filter through to their chosen subject or desk in
spite of the apparent formality of the parti, so the public
spaces dissipate into a 'capillary network' of access
routes to single family homes. While there is a highly
formal relationship between the mediatheque and town
hall, the locality's two most important public buildings,
that formality is softened and even made ambiguous by
the pervasive relationship between space, buildings and
nature.

Within this overall aim are what Perrault calls a
series of 'brushstrokes' – elements of a modest size,
like a gently sloping square on the corner of Gambetta
Street and Marcel Houel Avenue and an embankment
along the avenue – which suggest, rather than coerce,
patterns of use.

Perrault concludes: 'Our strategy is not to have one!
Or more precisely, not to believe in the good guesses of
our "beloved" urban planners. Instead, a living process
that thinks of the city piece by piece'. It is a vision made
all the more compelling by the extreme rigour and
rationalism of the forms, which achieve a remarkable
cohesion with the existing grain. It is, perhaps, an apt
vignette of the aim of the library building programme,
to offer means for personal fulfilment within the
formality of a public institution. ◬

Sean Stanwick describes a modern 'Cabinet of Wonders', commissioned from Toronto-based architect Johnson Chou by the filmmaker John Greyson.

The Toronto Arts Awards is an annual event where artists and designers are recognised for their achievements in various creative disciplines. Recipients are awarded a cash prize to commission a work from an emerging artist or designer. When filmmaker, and admitted collector of all things curious, John Greyson received the honour in November 2000, he called on Toronto designer Johnson Chou to create a modern cabinet to house his collection of diverse mementos. Chou's response, the Cabinet of Wonders, transcends the mere functionality requested by Greyson, and is as magical as it is delightfully seductive.

In its closed position, the uniform black lacquer surface gives the cabinet an iconic presence. Grant it a cursory review and the story might well end with its utilitarian appearance. Yet its apparent singularity of form belies the complexity and depth of the layering held within. It is only when the layers are peeled away that the multiplicity of its form becomes fully revealed. As the front panels pivot and roll away, translucent acrylic cells of varying shapes and sizes slide and rotate 360 degrees to fully expose their contents. Vitrines open, a multi-level glass cylinder extends outward, and a single cube, the only desire of which is to be revealed, rises from beneath a hidden recess to glow with a mystical radiance.

Our internal voyeur knows all too well that the beauty of seduction lies less in the revealed than in the act of revealing. More akin to an erotic piece of lingerie, the black wrapping and translucent outer skin does as much to conceal and then skilfully expose, as it does to define form. It is, in reality, a vehicle for sensory temptation, providing an enticing and suggestive glimpse of what has yet to be revealed. The radiant glow emanating from beneath its surfaces intentionally teases the senses and creates a state of excited anticipation as the magic unfolds before our eyes. But Chou, unwilling to simply observe, takes this notion one step further and grants us the joy of interactive participation. So often restricted to visual stimulation, our hands are invited to fully explore every inch of its tactile and visceral pleasures.

Gypsy Rose Lee used the power of visual temptation to popularise striptease in the 1930s, and it is a notion that permeates Chou's work as well. His fondness for transformation, penetration, and the resultant dematerialisation, is evident in several other works including Shade, which doubles as a wall-mounted display shelf and a source of ambient light.

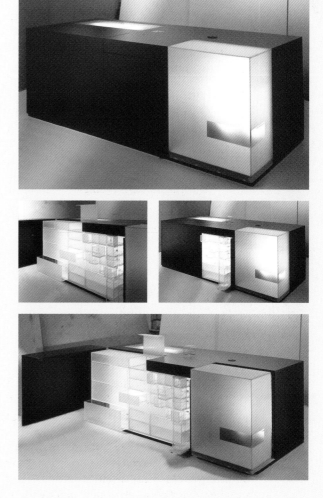

This doubleness of elements, the architectural proportions and theatrical use of light, lend an intentional urban-esque quality to much of Chou's work. Disregarding conventional notions of scale, The Cabinet of Wonders dances between the micro and macro, and renders the distinction between object and building moot. Similarities with the recent work of Modernist architects Herzog and de Meuron seem apparent; references Chou welcomes. 'My work is a constant critique of the built environment and the objects we live with', he says, 'there's nothing worse than a space that is mute'. Given his apparent comfort with the ambiguities of scale, and his mastery of light as a vehicle to inspire curiosity, this seems highly unlikely. ◿

Below top
Architects + Engineers = Structures,
Wiley-Academy, 2002.

Below bottom
Ivan Margolius with his inspirational
1949 Tatra 600 – Tatraplan.

Interview with Ivan Margolius

Abigail Grater talks to author Ivan Margolius about his new book for Wiley-Academy, *Architects + Engineers = Structures*.

The greatest contributions to the built environment are those structures that result from a synergy between the vision of the architect and the technical and intuitive skill of the engineer. It is a strange and unfortunate fact that the relationship between architect and engineer is often inclined to be tense and hierarchical. This is keenly felt by architect and author Ivan Margolius, whose latest book, *Architects + Engineers = Structures*, sets out to redress the balance by presenting innovative structures from a range of countries and periods which demonstrate the best of architect–engineer collaboration.

'Engineers are frowned upon by architects', he explains. 'Architects are rated over them, which is a shame because they contribute enormously – they are equal partners. In most books, only the architect is listed as the sole building designer. With Mies van der Rohe or Le Corbusier buildings, you never know who the engineer was. It took me a great amount of effort to find out who these people were, and sometimes I didn't succeed, because they were totally obscure. Those architects actually respected the engineers and worked with them on equal terms, but when historians wrote about them it was never picked up, so I thought it was a good idea to introduce the subject.'

Margolius emphasises that the relationship between architects and engineers relies on mutual understanding: 'It's very bad when people aren't open enough to cooperate. You are always trying to sketch out ideas, ask the engineer what he thinks, work round the table and see what can come out of it, rather than just do your design and give it to the engineer to calculate. Maybe the engineer will have a better idea, or maybe the architect will. Future Systems had the idea of this monocoque shell for the Lord's Cricket Ground, and asked the engineers how it could be done, to structure this egg-shaped form. Sometimes when you design a bridge the engineer will come up with a brilliant idea of how it can be supported, and you will follow his lead. It depends who's got the best idea'.

Margolius began his architectural career in the London-based practice Yorke Rosenberg Mardall (later YRM), returning there at various stages. Under the auspices of this firm he has been involved in a diverse range of projects, most notably Gatwick Airport – the masterplan and buildings of which, unusually for a project of this size and duration, have been overseen by the same firm since its inception in the late 1950s, giving it its current coherence. Here he played a key role in designing the North Terminal, rapid transit stations, a hotel and other buildings. Over the years he has also worked for other notable firms – Foster and

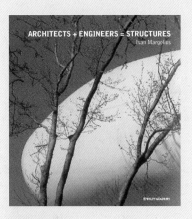

Partners; Koetter, Kim & Associates; Skidmore, Owings & Merrill – as well as being an associate in the smaller firm of McMillan West Faggetter, founded in 1972 by one of his colleagues at Yorke Rosenberg Mardall. This range of experience has given him an understanding of different design approaches, and while the constraints of a large firm are not always ideal for nurturing creative individuality, at Foster and Partners in particular his eyes were opened to innovation in building: 'They always looked at other technologies to see what they could use to transfer into architecture – aircraft, automobiles and other industries which would be able to help in resolving certain things like building skin, structure and shapes and forms'. He is now back at YRM for the third time, and seems set to stay.

His current settled position, living in a peaceful Bedfordshire village and working in YRM's elegant City offices, presents a sharp contrast with the traumas and upheavals of his early life. Born in Czechoslovakia in 1947, he narrowly missed the Second World War, during which his entire family had been held in concentration camps and his grandparents had perished. However, the ordeals that beset his family did not end there: his father, who held a position in the Czech government, was unlawfully executed after a stage trial during the persecutions of the 1950s. Margolius and his mother remained trapped by the oppressive Communist regime until, in 1966, the Czech borders were finally opened, and they fled to Britain.

Unable to find jobs, his mother and stepfather were forced to return to their native country after a month. Margolius himself was a student at the time of their flight, and had completed a year of architectural training at the Czech Institute of Technology in Prague. This eased his

Book covers: left to right
Cubism in Architecture and the Applied Arts, David & Charles, 1979
Tatra – The Legacy of Hans Ledwinka, SAF Publishing, 1990
Skoda Laurin & Klement, Osprey Automotive, 1992
Prague – a Guide to 20th-Century Architecture, second edition, Ellipsis-Könemann, 1996
Church of the Sacred Heart, Joze Plecnik, 1922–33, Phaidon Press, 1995
Automobiles by Architects, Wiley-Academy, 2000
Prague Farewell by Ivan Margolius's mother Heda Margolius Kovaly, third British edition, Indigo, 1997

transition into British life, as he was able to take up an architecture course at The Polytechnic in Regent Street (later the University of Westminster).

Margolius's experience of both Czech and British architectural education systems has arguably equipped him with a more balanced viewpoint than either system allows in isolation. In Czechoslovakia, at the time of his education, students obtained a joint architecture-engineering degree, for which a great deal of emphasis was placed on high mathematics and the creative process was secondary. In Britain, architecture and engineering were, and are, treated as separate disciplines. When he transferred to Britain, Margolius had to start again. He spent the first year of his training in London producing a model of a house that was methodically developed through considering light, sound, form and the activities of the people within it. He sees the positive aspects of both methods, acknowledging that the Czech course gave him a greater understanding and appreciation of structural engineering, while the London course encouraged functional considerations and aesthetic concerns.

A realisation that certain aspects of Czech culture had remained unknown outside the boundaries of the country through its long period of isolation led Margolius to begin his first publishing efforts. Soon after arriving in London, he had visited Foyles bookshop, spurred on by an interest in books that was inherited from his mother, who had translated various English texts including works by Raymond Chandler, John Steinbeck and HG Wells, into Czech. Browsing the bookshelves, a gaping hole became apparent to him: 'There wasn't anything there on the subjects that I knew about and which were important in Czech culture and Czech life, and I realised that people in Western Europe didn't know anything about it. So I thought maybe my task would be to try to write books which would help to deliver this information through the rest of the world'.

This he achieved, first with his book *Cubism in Architecture and the Applied Arts* (1979). Cubist architecture, despite its obvious relationship with the artistic developments in Western Europe, was a movement limited entirely to Bohemia, around 1910. No existing text in the West covered it; Reyner Banham and Kenneth Frampton were unaware of it when writing their accounts of modern architecture. Through Margolius's exposition, it received due international recognition, leading to added chapters in revised editions of

Banister Fletcher's architectural 'bible', *A History of Architecture*.

In 1990 and 1992 followed two acclaimed books on Czech motorcars: *Tatra – The Legacy of Hans Ledwinka* and *Skoda Laurin & Klement*. During preparation of the Tatra book, Margolius discovered that several Czech architects had designed cars for Tatra, and began to wonder how widespread was the relationship between car design and architecture. His consequent research, which uncovered automotive experiments by many of the world's most famous architects, led to his book *Automobiles by Architects* (2000), universally praised by critics for its combination of depth, readability and entertainment. In the interim period he had published two further books: one a popular pocket-sized volume on 20th-century architecture in Prague, the other on Slovenian architect Joze Plecnik's Church of the Sacred Heart.

Throughout his life Margolius has maintained a close friendship with Jan Kaplicky, a fellow Czech and founder of the innovative London architectural firm Future Systems. The two have worked together on the competition design of a memorial in Prague dedicated to those who lost their lives in the Communist regime. Margolius has also interviewed Kaplicky for book and magazine publications. Like Kaplicky, Margolius is fascinated with the influence of technology and art on architecture. He is now working on a forthcoming issue of *Architectural Design* entitled 'Art and Architecture', due out in Spring 2003. His next contribution to the broader spectrum of architectural writing is eagerly awaited. ⌂

Architects + Engineers = Structures (paperback, 104 pages, ISBN 0471498254, £19.99) and *Automobiles by Architects* (paperback, 160 pages, ISBN 047160786X, £29.95) are available from Customer Services Department, John Wiley & Sons Ltd, 1 Oldlands Way, Bognor Regis, West Sussex, PO22 9SA, Tel: 01243 843294, Fax: 01243 01243 843296, Email: cs-books@wiley.co.uk, Website: www.wiley.com or www.wileyeurope.com.

SPECIAL OFFER
Automobiles by Architects is available from John Wiley & Sons (details above) at a special price of £19.95 by quoting Offer ALK. Offer ends 31st December 2002.

Subscribe Now for 2002

As an influential and prestigious architectural publication, *Architectural Design* has an almost unrivalled reputation worldwide. Published bimonthly, it successfully combines the currency and topicality of a newsstand journal with the editorial rigour and design qualities of a book. Consistently at the forefront of cultural thought and design since the 1960s, it has time and again proved provocative and inspirational – inspiring theoretical, creative and technological advances. Prominent in the 1980s for the part it played in Post-Modernism and then in Deconstruction, ⌀ has recently taken a pioneering role in the technological revolution of the 1990s. With groundbreaking titles dealing with cyberspace and hypersurface architecture, it has pursued the conceptual and critical implications of high-end computer software and virtual realities. ⌀

⌀ Architectural Design

SUBSCRIPTION RATES 2002
Institutional Rate: UK £160
Personal Rate: UK £99
Discount Student* Rate: UK £70
OUTSIDE UK
Institutional Rate: US $240
Personal Rate: US $150
Student* Rate: US $105

*Proof of studentship will be required when placing an order. Prices reflect rates for a 2002 subscription and are subject to change without notice.

TO SUBSCRIBE
Phone your credit card order:
UK/Europe: +44 (0)1243 843 828
USA: +1 212 850 6645
Fax your credit card order to:
UK/Europe: +44 (0)1243 770 432
USA: +1 212 850 6021

Email your credit card order to:
cs-journals@wiley.co.uk
Post your credit card or cheque order to:

UK/Europe: John Wiley & Sons Ltd.
Journals Administration Department
1 Oldlands Way
Bognor Regis
West Sussex PO22 9SA
UK

USA: John Wiley & Sons Ltd.
Journals Administration Department
605 Third Avenue
New York, NY 10158
USA

Please include your postal delivery address with your order.

All ⌀ volumes are available individually. To place an order please write to:
John Wiley & Sons Ltd
Customer Services
1 Oldlands Way
Bognor Regis
West Sussex PO22 9SA

Please quote the ISBN number of the issue(s) you are ordering.

⌀ is available to purchase on both a subscription basis and as individual volumes

---

○ I wish to subscribe to ⌀ *Architectural Design* at the **Institutional rate of £160.**

○ I wish to subscribe to ⌀ *Architectural Design* at the **Personal rate of £99.**

○ I wish to subscribe to ⌀ *Architectural Design* at the **Student rate of £70.**

STARTING FROM ISSUE 1/2002.

○ Payment enclosed by Cheque/Money order/Drafts.

Value/Currency £/US$ [   ]

○ Please charge £/US$ [   ] to my credit card.
Account number:

[ ][ ][ ][ ][ ][ ][ ][ ][ ][ ][ ][ ][ ][ ][ ][ ]

Expiry date:

[ ][ ][ ][ ][ ]

Card: Visa/Amex/Mastercard/Eurocard *(delete as applicable)*

Cardholder's signature [   ]

Cardholder's name [   ]

Address [   ]

[   ]

[   ] Post/Zip Code [   ]

Recipient's name [   ]

Address [   ]

[   ]

[   ] Post/Zip Code [   ]

I would like to buy the following Back Issues at £22.50 each:

○ ⌀ 157 *Reflexive Architecture*, Neil Spiller

○ ⌀ 156 *Poetics, in Architecture*, Leon van Schaik

○ ⌀ 155 *Contemporary Techniques in Architecture*, Ali Rahim

○ ⌀ 154 *Fame and Architecture*, J. Chance and T. Schmiedeknecht

○ ⌀ 153 *Looking Back in Envy*, Jan Kaplicky

○ ⌀ 152 *Green Architecture*, Brian Edwards

○ ⌀ 151 *New Babylonians*, Iain Borden + Sandy McCreery

○ ⌀ 150 *Architecture + Animation*, Bob Fear

○ ⌀ 149 *Young Blood*, Neil Spiller

○ ⌀ 148 *Fashion and Architecture*, Martin Pawley

○ ⌀ 147 *The Tragic in Architecture*, Richard Patterson

○ ⌀ 146 *The Transformable House*, Jonathan Bell and Sally Godwin

○ ⌀ 145 *Contemporary Processes in Architecture*, Ali Rahim

○ ⌀ 144 *Space Architecture*, Dr Rachel Armstrong

○ ⌀ 143 *Architecture and Film II*, Bob Fear

○ ⌀ 142 *Millennium Architecture*, Maggie Toy and Charles Jencks

○ ⌀ 141 *Hypersurface Architecture II*, Stephen Perrella

○ ⌀ 140 *Architecture of the Borderlands*, Teddy Cruz

○ ⌀ 139 *Minimal Architecture II*, Maggie Toy

○ ⌀ 138 *Sci-Fi Architecture*, Maggie Toy

○ ⌀ 137 *Des-Res Architecture*, Maggie Toy